Experience

Heaven

on *Earth*

The New Matrix of Life

Salantra

"The Gem of Custom Book Publishing"
Outskirts Press, Inc.
Denver, Colorado

Experience Heaven on Earth: The New Matrix of Life
All Rights Reserved.
Copyright © 2008 *Salantra*
V2.0 R1.0

Cover Photo © 2008 Christine Bearse. All rights reserved - used with permission.

Illustrations by *Salantra,*
Christina Bryer, Bryan deFlores, and
to someone that prefers to remain anonymous.

Published by
Outskirts Press, Inc.
10940 S. Parker Rd. - 515
Parker, CO 80134

Outskirts Press is a publishing company harnessing the latest in technical advancements. By combining digital publishing-on-demand technology with online convenience, Outskirts Press brings the power of success back to the writer. We publish manuscripts and distribute high-quality paperback, hardback, and electronic format books from new and established writers alike and then provide the tools necessary to market successfully. Our cutting-edge digital process allows us to publish a great number of titles each year. Outskirts Press is a proud member of the Denver BBB and the Colorado Independent Publishers Association.

Elaine Salantra, 1944
Experience Heaven on Earth: *The New Matrix of Life* /*Salantra*
First Edition: 2008
Includes glossary

Printed on 30% recycled paper

Outskirts Press, Inc.
http://www.outskirtspress.com

ISBN: 978-1-4327-1984-5

Library of Congress Control Number: 2008923266

Outskirts Press and the "OP" logo are trademarks belonging to Outskirts Press, Inc.

PRINTED IN THE UNITED STATES OF AMERICA

Dedication:
for humanity

Dear Reader,

Experience Heaven on Earth contains a genuine spiritual message that prepares us for the new matrix of life. Its multidimensional perspective emanates all that we are as unified consciousness, which challenges us to liberate ourselves from archaic paradigms of organized teachings, and fully experience independent thinking. It underscores that as we embrace all that we are within consciousness, we give ourselves an opportunity to experience the grand scope of multidimensional life.

Our innate ability to ascend into the fullness of a new matrix of life requires that we transmute limited patterns of human conditioning. During this momentum of transformation it is crucial that we remember previous experiences and integrate them into our present-day awareness. As we embrace all that we are, we activate innate seeds of knowing that support us while we remember lifetimes of on- and off-planet experiences. Therefore, the more we assimilate the heightened awareness that is already part of our consciousness, the more we energetically feel our own resonance of light.

Throughout this book the avoidance of the word "I" as a personal reference is intentional, so that as we energetically feel the frequency that accompanies the words, egoic-response is minimized. Our conscious use of the words *we* and *our*, transmutes any imbalanced intention and integrates the concept of unity into our awareness. Any reference to *you* and *your* intentionally directs you inward and brings the learning home. Also, the deliberate use of lower case, energetically supports equality and spiritual communion as in: jeshua, christ, al-mahdi, creator, god, source, yhvh, shekinah, yhsvh, all-that-is, ain soph or and names such as those of archangels, star systems, planets, ages of light, months and so on.

In order to facilitate your ascension experience, this book contains energetic keys that sustain advanced frequencies of light, which ground the past and the future into your present reality. It is highly recommended that you assimilate these frequencies at a pace that works for you. The more you experience each of these keys, the more you amplify your frequency, so it is crucial that you use them with absolute integrity. As you become more aware of your own resonant pulsation of light you experience inner communion with all that you are as unified consciousness.

The encodements of light within this book facilitate those lifestreams ready to experience the true lineage of their intergalactic origin. In support of this heightened perspective I trust that every individual that is guided to read it energetically feels their own transformation and assimilation of consciousness.

If you would like to know more about the new matrix of multidimensional life, please visit my new website, www.HeavenOnEarthInternational.com.

Many blessings,

salantra

Matrix for Content

Matrix of Geometric Encodements of Light

Blueprint of the 5ᵗʰ Dimensional Circuit System

Consciousness on the New Earth

New Encodement Within the Heavens

Matrix of Life on the New Earth

Keys: Matrix for Synergy

Matrix of Illustrations

Foreword

The sacred geometric symbol on the front cover of this book contains an intergalactic message.

As part of my journey of awakening, a few years ago, I was granted the ability to travel to the akashic records to bring forth personal sacred geometric symbols. Early in the spring of 2006, Salantra, a dear spiritual sister and personal friend asked me to bring forth, if possible, a geometric symbol to represent her book, one that she began writing in august of 1999. And, as this book is a living language of light, it naturally made sense to me that there is a specific symbol that would transmit its interstellar encodement. The frequency, that is this symbol, came through me on 10-16-2006.

The stars and the sky have been a source of wondrous inner recognition of home, my entire life. Several years ago, while in a meditative state of awareness, divine grace supported me as I lifted another layer of veils within my own consciousness. I experienced full communion with my galactic lineage as I met my star mother, who is from pleaides and my star father, from sirius b. To this day, we have wonderful conversations with each other.

When I enter a meditative state to go into the akashic records, I am met by my star parents. One of the ways they serve me during these experiences is as escorts to the staircase that leads to this sacred temple. My star father then transmits an inner knowing that guides me to the location within the temple. In this case, the destination was salantra¹s akashic records, which contain the frequency of light that emanates the symbol for this book.

Normally a symbol takes approximately 1 hour to complete, yet for whatever reason this one took 2 hours to fully emerge onto paper. While engaged in this particular meditative state, I completely lost track of time, feeling and sensing a multitude of energetic experiences that cannot be defined. An aspect of the spiritual connection that Salantra and I have with one another as intergalactic sisters is that we support each other while on earth. In this book, Salantra translates her frequency as a living language of light and puts it into a conscious form through words. I am honored to facilitate her in this endeavor, and retrieve this geometric symbol from her records to express the language of light, without words.

As you read this book you will receive your own experience of self-realization, self-actualization. All that we are, within, is indeed the source of all that we seek. May this symbol enhance and contribute to your own inner journey.

Peace

christine bearse
www.awakeningrainbows.com
wethersfield, ct

With Deep Gratitude

There are some special people in my life who, over the last several years have facilitated in bringing this book to fulfillment. I would like to express my sincere gratitude to each of you.

To my dear friend maryellen malak madden, thank you for your continuous unconditional support and devoted service to the highest good of all. To joseph buscema and wendy rieker, a special heartfelt thank you, for applying your talents to assist in the shift of my vibrational frequency. Together, maryellen, joseph and wendy, you set the stage for the completion of this book.

To sylvia davi, a lifelong friend and creator of exquisite life coaching, thank you for your support and editing assistance in translating the language of light into layman terms. You helped me to remain grounded and maintain focus so that clarity comes forth even during the throws of this creative endeavor.

To christine bearse, a companion traveler who fully supports me through all of my earth experiences, my loving heartfelt gratitude to you, for your innate ability to energetically feel my frequency. Through your artistic creativity you bring forth the final energetic capstone for this book—the geometric image for the front cover. Dear spirit sister we are both consciously aware of the energetic connection we share throughout eternity.

To ann and jay hardy, loving and supportive friends, your kinship is very precious to me. Thank you for being in my life and for your technical computer assistance throughout this endeavor. To bev schenler, thank you, with all my heart, for your sincere dedication during a significant phase of this creative endeavor. To diane warren, thank you for your assistance during the preliminary stage of this writing.

To christina bryer, artist for the interstellar design of the platonic solid, icosa-dodecahedron, thank you for your permission to use this geometric symbol in my book. To celia fenn, international spiritual facilitator for the ascension experience, my sincere appreciation for connecting me with your friend, christina. Although the 3 of us have yet to personally meet in this life, my thoughts hold deep gratitude for the spiritual direction that reconnects us once again.

To outskirts press, inc., my appreciation to you for maintaining a high level of integrity in bringing its publication to completion. To my author representative, lisa hendrix, my deepest heartfelt gratitude to you, for your endless support in caring enough to make sure that this book is published in the way inner guidance intended. It brings me great joy to meet you again and with honor, participate in another soul contract. To the graphic arts department at outskirts press, and especially to sonya woods, thank you for your assistance with the art images. To someone that prefers to remain anonymous, you are an angel. To you, my deepest expression of gratitude for creating the final images for the illustrations as well as the layout for the cover design.

To another special friend and spiritual brother, bryan deflores, founder of lightquest international llc, and the academy of intergalactic science and wisdom, thank you for the geometric encodement of light that you bring into the 3rd dimension through your artistic creativity. On a more personal note bryan, my deepest appreciation for our energetic connection and for drawing the geometric blueprint of my galactic lightbody. On this drawing is the image of a book.

The more we synergize our resonant pulsation of light,
the more we experience all that we are,
as unified consciousness on the new earth.

Quantum Shift Into Another Age of Light

Transfiguration in Consciousness

Humanity's ascension is a universal experience and its transfiguration in consciousness is essential to the new matrix of life. As a human race, we give credence to this welcomed paradigm as it transfigures eons of human conditioning and encourages a new declaration of inner liberation, one in which we experience ultimate freedom and independent thinking.

The new matrix of life transfigures 3rd dimensional limitation, which blindly follows organized teachings that reinforce archaic beliefs. The hidden message in most of these teachings implies that the only way to experience the presence of god is to continue to support these beliefs. For jews, this belief is known as the return of the messiah; for christians, it is known as the second-coming of christ; for muslims, al-mahdi. By any name these beliefs subtly reinforce the illusion of separation. In truth, unified consciousness extends beyond form, concept, time and space, and emanates cosmic intelligence as our resonance of inner knowing.

As separation unifies a multidimensional understanding filters into our awareness. While we consciously remember all that we are as unified consciousness, the human need for external reliance upon sacred sources such as, gurus, angels, spirit guides, ascended masters, and so on, transfigures. Therefore, as we experience the momentum of this immense shift, we consciously transcend indoctrination and come together by way of an innate spiritual connection that is accessible and real. Actually, as we synergize matter and spirit the seen and unseen unify.

As our consciousness transfigures we experience synchronicity with our inner guidance system, which aligns our awareness with the totality of all-that-is. We reference creator, source, universe, omni verse, *I AM, yhvh* [yah veh], *shekinah* [sh' ki nah], and *yhsvh* [yah hesh'ua], as our own resonant pulsations of light that transcend our personified perspectives of separation into a balanced understanding of all that we are as unified consciousness.

1

In the new matrix of life we are a timeless divine blueprint, formless yet all form, as we consciously live in the nothing and everything simultaneously. The geometric codes in this blueprint emanate an advanced spectrum of light into the nucleus of every atom and cell of all life. Therefore, as the essence of all-that-is, we use the stars as our eyes, the wind as our eternal breath, the rivers and oceans as our cosmic bloodstream, the sounds of nature as the answer to our spiritual call, and transmit the spoken word *I AM* through our voice.

✿　✿　✿

Place your feet firmly on the ground.... Envision the night sky, and lift your head towards it.... Fix your eyes on the stars that glow in your vision.... Intuitively sense the wind as your eternal breath.... Feel the rivers and oceans as your cosmic bloodstream.... Listen to the sounds of nature as your spiritual call, and energetically feel your resonance of light as you declare the following spoken word....

✿　✿　✿

"Within the radiant sun,
I AM the light of god.
Through the breeze of the wind,
I AM the eternal breath of god.
As the ebb and flow of the ocean's tides,
I AM the bloodstream of god.
In the silence of nature,
I AM in full presence with god.
Within the heart of all life,
I AM in communion, as god."

✿　✿　✿

Perception Beyond Human Individuality

Evolution within consciousness occurs when all-that-is experiences its perfection through human individuation. The full scope of this multidimensional perspective requires that we expand our perception beyond human individuality, and internalize an advanced concept that defines life in accordance with our full human potential.

As we create the way in which we fulfill our quantum shift to the new matrix of life, many lifestreams are unaware of the greater spiritual gains that would be theirs by transforming their perception so that it expands beyond all human limitation.

The more we claim our divine birthright, the more we consciously integrate advanced levels of awareness and energetically experience the flexibility within abstract thought forms. Our new perception gives way to the knowing that we are intergalactic emissaries from civilizations far beyond earth's galaxy, experiencing human embodiment on earth.

While living on earth we have the opportunity to evolve through our own humanness and bring forth full conscious awareness of our experiences from timelines in other interplanetary civilizations. As we expand our awareness beyond our own individuality, we realize that we have the innate ability to perceive multidimensional inclusiveness. The extent, to which we bridge the gap between the heart and the higher mind, enables us to energetically feel our own resonant pulsation of light in other interplanetary civilizations.

Principle of Conscious Preference

The art of living in physical embodiment without the framework of human conditioning requires that we evaluate our belief system, and transmute our limiting beliefs and thoughts into a heightened state of awareness. In doing so, we redefine our beliefs so that we take the essential action that facilitates new direction in our life.

As we experience the momentum of the quantum shift our lives appear to be out of control. This is essential so that we remember and become conscious enough to let go of the old. Being conscious requires that we are aware of everything around us so that we can make effective choices in our day-to-day life.

The more we expand our awareness, the more we transmute the old paradigm of choice into a conscious preference. The underlying principle of initiating a heightened inclination signifies that we are responsible for the chain of events that affect us internally and externally. This awareness requires that we tune into and energetically feel the outcome of our preferences so that we discern whether we want to continue to initiate a particular experience.

Every conscious preference emanates a vibration that streams outward into infinity; therefore, through our own projection we receive what we intend. *As creators, we actualize experience.*

Conscious Knowing Emerges

Conscious knowing is an immediate recognition of energetic transmissions that originate beyond our intellect. It is the result of the fusion of light in our heart, and we energetically feel it as an intuitive inspiration that comes before the perception of rational awareness.

As our awareness deepens we experience inner conflict between our intuition and intellect. The heart reveals specific direction and the mind intentionally contradicts it by implying an opposing perspective. The more we neutralize all opposition from the mind, the more we enable intuition to lead our intellect through what we energetically feel and intuitively know. The more our intuition and intellect work together as natural partners, the more conscious knowing solidifies within our awareness.

We experience balance from within and fully comprehend the innate awareness that emerges in every moment. We bring a new paradigm into the forefront—we accept that inner communion with all that we are, as god, is the ultimate potential of human experience.

Infinite Love

Without limits or barriers, the immense adoration of infinite love emanates as our light, yet this essence of our own resonant pulsation of light radiates to our consciousness in other star systems, galaxies and universes.

In the new matrix of life the endless pulsation of this innate love directs the way to gratitude, stability, peace, equality, divinity, synergy and synchronicity. The more we live in accordance with the divine plan, the more we experience heartfelt kinship with others.

Earth's Quantum Shift

During the momentum of earth's quantum shift, transfiguration in consciousness and form is so immense that our human mind is unable to fully perceive its impact on our lives. As earth forges into another era of light, it completes an essential cosmic alignment in its star system. This grand alignment facilitates in the further ascension of other planets and stars, in every galaxy and universe.

According to the mayan calendar, in 2012, earth attains its perfected cosmic alignment as it assumes its rightful position within the grand scheme of interplanetary alignment. It completes a 26,000 year cycle and participates in a major quantum shift within the cosmos. In fact this event begins in the linear year 1994 with earth's entry into what is known as the photon belt, and while in this enlightened phase earth assimilates photonic light for the next 2000 years. Therefore, this cosmic belt of light supports earth's transfiguration into its perfected state, as the new earth.

The interstellar qualities within this photon belt manifest a profound force field that lowers earth's magnetics to the point where ultimately, earth accelerates the speed of its revolution so that its ascension happens naturally. This occurs under the direction of the divine plan as it aligns earth with its new position in the cosmos. As earth moves through this imminent process, it attains fulfillment of its destiny.

During the momentum of earth's transition changes in its magnetic grid system create geological shifts, thinning of the ozone layer, unusual fluctuations in atmospheric pressure, and global warming, which is a direct result of the increase in greenhouse gases found in glaciers and polarized regions. Scientists state that human activity is primarily responsible for the rise in earth's temperature and that carbon dioxide concentration is due to the use of fossil fuel, while the increase in methane and nitrous oxide is due to 3rd dimensional agricultural practices.

Increase in arctic temperatures and the melting of its snow and ice cause oceans to expand and rise. As earth's air and ocean temperatures elevate, heavy rainfalls are more frequent in many areas, affecting seawater salinity, wind patterns, precipitation, drought, heat waves and tropical cyclones.

Transfiguration in earth's magnetic grid manifests as geological and atmospheric events, which facilitate planetary purification of pollutants and dissonance. Natural geological events occur in earth's substructure and atmosphere, and create earthquakes, volcanic eruptions, hurricanes, tornados and tsunamis for the purpose of cleansing earth and further acceleration of its ascension. These natural occurrences create electrical outages, water contamination, as well as periodic food and fuel shortages.

As earth aligns with its interstellar pulsation in the galactic core all life forms feel the effects of this quantum shift.

As we pioneer the new matrix of life
we live as unified consciousness.

Ascension Into the New Matrix of Life

Overview of the New Matrix of Life

The new matrix of life is profoundly different than other eons of human existence. The more we experience this cohesive state of awareness, the more we synergize all that we are as unified consciousness. Based in absolute equality, this new matrix emanates a seed of awareness that fans the flame of divinity within us, so that we awaken to the innate presence of the androgynous principles, yhvh and shekinah. As we remember our divinity we use the spoken word; such as, *I AM* and *binah ruach devekut* [b-nah roo'-ach dev-e-koot'], to sense the essence of yhsvh as our own resonant pulsation of light. In accordance with divine timing, we awaken to this awareness, and consciousness transfigures on a global scale.

The new matrix of life sustains abstract realities where we unify our intellect and experience flexibility and adaptability. It redefines our awareness as its frequency sweeps through us like a tsunami that floods us with the waters of purification, rejuvenation and complete restoration. It synergizes the individualized fields of knowledge throughout religion, science and spirituality. And, it creates essential transformation in these institutions, as well as in the systems of health, education, economics, government, environment, technology, transportation, community, and the role of race and creed within society. The initial impact of this multidimensional threshold is just the tip of the iceberg, and our transition to this new way of life is so immense that the breakdown of these systems alters our physical, cerebral, emotional and material stability.

Even though some of us have glimpses of how this quantum shift transforms our lives, nothing is as it appears to be; therefore, it is virtually impossible to foresee the grand picture as we establish a new foundation in the unknown. What some of us know for certain is that although this unfamiliar reality appears invisible in 3rd dimensional density, it is real and acceptance of this awareness is a major key to our future.

For most of us the concept of living in the new matrix of life is new and it requires that we remember all that we are as unified consciousness. In truth, this new matrix awakens the cords of intergalactic awareness, as if to say, "ah yes, remembrance of this resonant pulsation of light is familiar." The more we synthesize our light in this intangible reality the easier it is to celebrate the joy of its familiarity.

The degree of acceleration that we attain within our circuit system determines our adaptability to the magnitude of living on the new earth. As our physiological circuitry increases its vibratory rate, and fully assimilates the interstellar substance ether, we amplify our sensory perceptions and synergize all separation in consciousness. Inner communion while in human embodiment brings our awareness home to wherever we are on earth, and once attained we live in synchronicity with all life.

The new matrix of life supports a balanced lifestyle of equality. We attain a heightened understanding of life through different phases of awareness; such as, awakening, activation, ascension, assimilation, conscious creation, manifestation, certainty, divinity and sovereignty. We claim our divine birthright, create a new life contract, heal indifference and align free will with divine will so that what we envision we fully manifest. We actualize liberation and divinity as well as experience unity through unlimited creativity, joy, abundance, truth, clarity, certainty, balance and infinite love.

As pioneers we are hallmarks for the new matrix of life and fully experience all that we are on the new earth. We:

✡ ✡ ✡

Expand our perceptions beyond individuality.

Complete soul contracts.

Convey responsibility and integrity.

Develop communities with balanced lifestyles.

Radiate infinite love.

Apply the spoken word.

Integrate the language of light.

Emanate our own resonant pulsation of light.

Live our full potential on the new earth.

Emanate mastery.

Live in awe of everything, and

Expect the unexpected, as constant change is the only stable condition.

✡ ✡ ✡

Conscious Language Shapes Reality

Language determines our full stream of consciousness from lifetime to lifetime, until we integrate the ultimate challenge of neutralizing its imbalanced effect. The application of conscious language accelerates our awareness and transfigures density, negativity and insufficiency. Therefore, words such as let, may, can, can't, should, need, try, if, but, no and not limit our ability to consciously create the reality that we choose to experience.

In the new matrix of life the use of conscious language shapes reality and the spoken word reinforces reality. Words spoken with clear intention consciously manifest the resonance of light it contains; therefore, it is essential that we are fully conscious of our language and how it creates the reality in which we live. The use of present tense transcends all imbalances in our verbal communication; therefore, all that appears abstract are tangible and the invisible is visible. We synthesize the present tense within our awareness every time we consciously declare the spoken word, *I AM.*

There is a fine distinction between "I" that is egoic in nature and "I" that is our omnipresent essence, as god. Without conscious awareness we use the egoic "I" as a point of reference to ego and the characteristics of its personality. With conscious awareness we intuitively sense the frequency of the word "I" as a reflection of all that we are as unified consciousness. Symbolic of its 3 lines: the vertical line, which connects the upper and lower horizontal lines, represents you; the upper horizontal line symbolizes heaven (spirit) and the lower horizontal line synthesizes earth (matter). The resonance of light within these 3 lines are essential to one another as they energetically synchronize so that "I" (you) experience yourself as the witnessing presence of all-that-is.

In the new matrix of life, we are the authentic living light of the *one*, rather than a dense reflection of the egoic "I."

Golden Age Terminology

This chart defines some key words and phrases that assist us in understanding the basics of golden age terminology. For additional awareness on these terms an expanded glossary is provided at the back of this book.

Ascension—upward mobility along a vertical axis; assimilation of the original configuration of dna; final phase of life on earth as we know it; divine birthright; integration of divinity; conscious mastery;

Blueprint—divine plan of creation; geometric grid of light that sustains encodements, as in 12-configurations of original dna; geometric design that holds patterns of light; sustains templates from which matrices are created;

Consciousness—energetic umbrella for a multitude of frequencies; infinite awareness of one's existence;

Electron particle spin—energetic momentum of particles in the main power current of our spinal column that transfigures frequencies of light; pulsating resonance in the center of the vesica piscis, a sacred symbol for 2 overlapping discs of light;

5th Dimension—heightened awareness in consciousness; new blueprint that sustains frequencies of geometric encodements;

Gold-platinum light—resonant pulsation of light that amplifies the electron particle spin in the central meridian of the spinal column; highest frequency of light that our physical body can synergize while in the 3rd dimension;

Interplanetary civilizations—our consciousness in other universes, galaxies and their star systems;

Interstellar—between or among the stars;

Intrastellar—within or inside a star or stars;

Lifestream—soul in embodiment; resonant frequency of light in other interplanetary civilizations; consciousness as it weaves within and throughout dimensions, star systems, galaxies and universes;

Matrix—an energetic projection of holographic light that solidifies through conscious intention; grids of light that sustain interstellar substance; facsimile of dimensional templates modulated into matrices of light; transfigures the core of each atom, sustains the molecule and cell of all life;

Resonant frequency—sensitivity to various wavelengths of light;

Resonant pulsation—our resonance of light as it flows throughout the main power current of our circuit system;

Solar heart— energetic distributor of light; sustains the interstellar elixir of infinite love; cosmic cadence that emanates from the galactic core or central sun; cosmic cadence, as our own pulsating rhythm, located behind and to the right of the physical heart; interstellar frequency of the unified heart within consciousness; sacred inner chamber of light where we energetically feel heightened states of awareness;

Synchronicity—energetic current through which we experience ease and grace in the flow of life; solidifies the intersection of all parallel realities; experience of realities that are parallel to the one moment;

Template—fixed pattern of light; the basis from which frequencies modulate patterns of light and manifest as individualized matrices through conscious intention;

Unified circuit system— complex system that infuses with the meridians in our physiological circuitry by way of the central nervous system to the brain; functions as one unit to energetically balance our body's electric, magnetic, neuralgic and subtle systems; includes physiological circuitry, cerebral-emotional circuitry, chakratic circuitry, subtle circuitry and the galactic lightbody; a reference point for the stabilization process, which supports the essential phase of inner communion;

Unified consciousness— communion of consciousness in all dimensions, star systems, galaxies and universes.

Conscious Ascension Now

Everything moves towards a turning point where the out-breath and in-breath of creation emanates from within.

As we experience the momentum of this turning point, the gap widens between lifestreams who claim their divine birthright and those who cling to the illusion of the material world. Through our choice to fully attain our own advanced state of awareness it is essential that we live in accordance with the divine plan. In doing so, we maintain our threshold of new found awareness and create a brand new foundation for life on the new earth. Although we give ourselves a huge challenge, it is through the mastery of inner conflict that we accomplish this task.

In truth, our soul level contract to be on earth during the time of this momenteous occasion, awakens the remembrance of all that we are and brings conscious knowing and action into balance with one another. This takes place in every moment, in every dimension and in every octave of light in each dimension—even beyond the 13 dimensions discussed later in this book. As consciousness ascends a domino effect radiates throughout the cosmos and transformation occurs on earth. Therefore, our ability to ascend into the new matrix of life is in direct relationship to how we overcome lifetimes of imperfect creations set into motion throughout eons of human embodiment.

As our civilization makes this massive transformation, there are 12 energetic waves of impetus during the ascension process, 6 of which facilitate humanity through this transition. Within these 6 waves, the 1st and 2nd waves support the new teachers for the 7th golden age. The 3rd and 4th support those lifestreams who assist the teachers. The 5th and 6th waves support both teachers and helpers as they implement new systems and concepts that sustain multidimensional frequencies of light. As an added note, during the momentum of this quantum shift the other 6 waves remain dormant.

A conscious understanding of these waves is actually beyond what our human mind can comprehend. And, at the time of this writing this concept has yet to fully manifest on earth. To assist us with our comprehension of these waves, the television and movie industries offer the intuitive knowing of how to project the impending reality of earth's purification, as well as portray our interaction with life in interplanetary civilizations. These industries hire writers that receive intergalactic transmissions, and bring awareness that is normally unconscious into a conscious physical reality. Every transmission sustains specific encodements of cosmic intelligence; therefore, as we assimilate these codes they activate conscious understanding of communion with the true lineage of our intergalactic origin. While we assimilate the many phases of inner communion, it is essential that we energetically feel or sense the momentum of these waves, otherwise we are unable to complete our ascension.

Some of these waves activate their momentum in the early 1980's with the continuous embodiment of many souls who incarnate as crystal children. These children are fully conscious of their light, emanate phenomenal intelligence and have complete knowing as to how the fulfillment of the quantum shift manifests on the new earth. They know that their purpose is to facilitate mass levels of change, in order to restructure essential systems necessary for the new matrix of life. Parental or adult programming is unable to override their inner connectedness and convictions, for these children know their own mastery. In the precise moment of the shift, their innate awareness of highly developed energetic technologies assist us so that we are fully present for the final moment of truth. Are you aware that these children are the ones who uphold the future for the new earth?

If we reject the ultimate experience of our conscious ascension, our soul finds an effective way to make its transition from the body before the shift occurs, or we teleport to another planet that is behind in human evolution in order to complete the cycle of 3rd dimensional life.

As we make the quantum shift the following principles ignite the fire for life on the new earth:

✿   ✿   ✿

Acceptance creates inner freedom.
Authenticity is the voice of truth.
Clarity emanates knowing.
Gratitude creates humility.
Infinite love is all there is.
Joy ignites the fire of passion.
Responsibility reveals integrity.
Destiny manifests as true purpose.

✿   ✿   ✿

Indicators of Ascension

Ascension creates physiological changes in our body and affects each of us regardless of our spiritual evolution. What then happens to our physical body during our experience of conscious ascension?

Our physical body is a dense reflection of a 3rd dimensional holding vessel for light as well as being cosmic in nature for the subtle frequencies within our unified circuit system. This unified system sustains a grid of light, which acts as a transducer that conducts the cosmic flow throughout our physiological circuitry. We energetically feel the frequencies within this complex system as our own resonant pulsations of light that flow throughout our physiological and cerebral-emotional circuitry. As these waves synergize their individualized frequencies into one unit of energy, we energetically feel the pulsation within this unified system of light throughout our physical body.

As synergy occurs, extreme physiological changes modify the cells and molecules in our circuit system, stimulate emotional clearing and shift the way we experience time, memory, orientation, appetite, sensitivity, tolerance and the familiar. These changes serve as indicators that ascension is at hand and sustain a new dynamic, which requires that we access our living temple of light and transmute imbalanced energy from our body. As we experience the momentum of our ascension, a restructuring of thought and emotion accelerates changes in the endocrine glands and activates detoxification, which transmutes environmental chemicals and food-borne toxins. If necessary, natural purification of our physiological circuitry manifests as energetic patterns of disease and as our ascension process hastens, purification lessens and most of these patterns eventually disappear.

The more we align our physical body to 5th dimensional frequencies, the more the molecules and cells transform, so that refinement occurs throughout our circuit system. As this transpires we feel momentary disorientation and out-of-sync with life. Short-term memory is unavailable in the moment, and intermittent disorientation takes place with reference to the day and time of day.

As we adapt to our accelerated frequency, we feel a clear, expansive flow of energy within our physical body and assimilate this rate of vibration throughout our circuit system. We consciously attune our awareness to the ever-changing indicators of ascension and ultimately experience stamina, require less sleep, change our eating habits and feel energetic charges as they flow through our circuitry. At this point in our ascension, we realize that transformation is visibly evident.

The following overview outlines some indicators of ascension in our physiological circuitry:

Bodily symptoms—headaches, sore or itchy scalp, rapid hair growth, sinus pressure, eye irritation, blurred vision, back and neck pain, pain between the shoulder blades, lymphatic congestion, rashes, heart palpitations, difficulty breathing, nausea and digestive difficulties. We transmute these blocked energies as we amplify our electron particle spin to a higher vibrational resonance of light;

Fatigue—as our body transmutes extreme physical and cerebral-emotional patterns, it loses 3rd dimensional density, undergoes great changes and requires additional periods of rest and reflection;

Intolerance—experience for lifestreams who pursue dense perspectives and engage in superficial conversations, which convey unhealthy attitudes and judgments, and ultimately manifest disharmonious events;

Emotional chaos—fluctuations in energy create emotional ups and downs, as well as generate feelings of disorientation, bewilderment and confusion;

Sleep requirements—fluctuate between interrupted sleep and long periods of deep sleep. Less sleep indicates adjustments to our internal clock, as our days and nights reverse. More sleep signifies that intense work occurs in the etheric realm;

Memory loss—as we experience the momentum of ascension memory loss manifests in epidemic proportions. There are many causes that contribute to this, one of which is electromagnetic disturbances from the impact of solar flare activity. This results in temporary energetic disruptions throughout earth's grid, which affects the core of its magnetic field. In addition, these disruptions interfere with receptors in the brain and interrupt the transfer of memory from short-term to long term. Restoration of memory requires the use of advanced forms of energetic technology, which makes us immune to these electromagnetic disturbances. The more we restore our energetic connection to all that we are as source, we maintain our memory through accelerated neurotransmitters in the brain;

Lightheadedness and loss of balance—as we move through our own revolving door to the new matrix of life, we literally bump into walls, as well as experience difficulty walking in a straight line;

Nobody home—as the momentum of the ascension process quickens, our body, mind and spirit require time to catch up to the shift that occurs energetically. As we integrate the ascension process our consciousness drifts in and out of our present awareness until the moment that soul completely descends into human embodiment;

Change in appetite—ascension requires an enormous amount of fuel and greater intake of food, often accompanied by an immediate need for satisfying hunger. The body requires different and perhaps unusual foods, in varying quantities, as it moves farther along the ascension process. It is essential that you trust that your body knows what it requires;

Energetic symptoms—sensation of head expansion, inner vision of the color red when eyes are closed, visual energetic perception, high-pitched auditory tones (ringing in the ears), external or internal trembling and tingling in extremities are also indicators that ascension is at hand;

Hypersensitivity—ascension creates hypersensitivity to external and internal surroundings and temporarily generates a sense of energetic overwhelm;

Life in the unknown—the familiar way we know ourselves shifts as our light penetrates the veil that separates the known from the unknown. As we become aware of the unknown our quality of life enhances profoundly. Our eyes see truth and we realize that the material world is the familiar illusion;

Quickened momentum—everything within and around us moves at warp speed;

As we cross the base threshold of ascension, we clear the slate and make room for newness in our lives. This point of no-return is where we begin to amplify the frequency of our electron particle spin and enter into what appears as the unknown, yet is so familiar. Are you ready to cross your base threshold?

Key: Cross the Threshold

To help you initiate the first step in crossing the threshold into the new matrix of life, your life force must amplify in frequency and pulsate at a minimum of 100,000 vibrations per mono-second. This pulsation enables you to energetically experience an alchemical elixir known as the breath of spiritual nectar.

✪　✪　✪

Place the tip of your tongue on the roof of your mouth, and slide it as far back on the upper palate as possible.... While your tongue is in this position focus your awareness on the back of your throat.... Breathe through your throat, until each breath sounds like an echo of wind as it passes through the back palate.... In this moment, be fully present with your physical body as it begins to feel lighter....

While in this slightly altered state, shift your awareness to the center of the earth-star, 6-12 inches below the arches of your feet.... Integrate your awareness into this energetic gateway, then inhale your life force upward along the spinal column to the top of your head.... Be present with your energy as it passes through your head, especially if you hear a popping sound in your ears....

Intuitively sense the energetic pulsation of your life force, as it flows through the crown of your head, and assimilate it into the soul-star, 6-12 inches above the top of your head.... Exhale your life force down the front of your physical body to the center of the earth-star below the arches of your feet.... Repeat this cycle of breath until you energetically feel the pulsation of your life force as it flows upward through the central meridian of your spinal column, and down the front of your body....

Shift your awareness to the solar heart, and energetically feel the pulsation of its cosmic cadence located behind and to the right of your human heart....

Intuitively sense its frequency as your own heart-based resonance of solar light.... Be fully present with the rhythm of your breath....

Envision a rose-quartz crystal bridge that leads to the new matrix of life, and step onto this bridge.... As you walk across this bridge, you pass through a pillar of violet-white light.... Continue to walk to the other end of the bridge, and once you reach it, energetically feel your own resonance of light as it flows within you, and pulsates at a minimum of 100,000 vibrations per mono-second....

When ready, bring your awareness out of your sacred heart chamber, and express gratitude for your experience.... Breathe into your new resonance of light, and assimilate its pulsation into your physiological circuitry....

✫   ✫   ✫

Ascension and the Electron Particle Spin

Science describes how each substance is defined by its unique atomic structure, and how each atom and molecule vibrates to a mathematical frequency. This frequency is quantified as a vibratory rate of speed expressed in terms of cycles per second. As science continues its advancement in measuring these frequencies, it further verifies that thoughts and feelings have energetic qualities that interact with these cycles.

All life reflects an original vibratory rate of energy that pulsates to repetitive cycles of lower or higher frequencies. Heightened states of awareness create corresponding changes in the range of these vibrational frequencies; therefore, ascension is an energetic acceleration that synthesizes a new encodement into our atoms, molecules and cells. The amplification of vibratory rate throughout the circuit system occurs during the assimilation of light, which sustains frequencies measured as vibrations per mono-second—1 mono-second is equal to 1 billionth of a second. As our electron particles synergize the full spectrum of light, our frequency amplifies to the highest vibration per mono-second available to us in the moment. We energetically feel these vibrations as waves of light that flow throughout our physiological circuitry. This information is based on conscious knowing, personal experience and familiarity with the transmission of vibrational frequencies, rather than the capability of science to measure.

A multidimensional energetic tool that we can use to amplify our electron particle spin is the spiritual symbol, the vesica piscis. This symbol is comprised of 2 overlapping discs of light, and when we place an image of this symbol at the coccyx and energetically spin its discs, we feel movement in the central meridian of our spinal column. As we become proficient in the appropriate use of this sacred symbol, we energetically feel our own resonance of light as it flows through this main power current. The electron particles in our physiological circuitry assimilate a heightened encodement and in that moment our consciousness activates several thresholds of awareness.

In the 1st phase of ascension we cross an initial spiritual threshold and awaken to the concept that life exists beyond the physical realm. Our light activates the life force at the base of our spinal column, and we energetically feel this energetic force move throughout the main power current. This momentum of energy activates our electron particle spin at a minimum of 100,000 vibrations per mono-second, which enables us to experience the breath of spiritual nectar. As we amplify our particle spin to 200,000 vibrations, we energetically feel the innate presence of soul and remember soul contracts with others.

From 300,000 to 400,000 vibrations per mono-second, we transfigure the core imprint of our belief system, neutralize thoughtforms and assimilate memories from our cellular circuitry. At this frequency we also amplify our electron particle spin and assimilate threads of our consciousness that project energetic cords of attachment.

At 500,000 vibrations, we energetically feel our own resonant pulsation of light within the spoken word. As we amplify our particle spin to 600,000, we clear our grid system with our own resonant frequency of the violet flame. Further amplification of our electron particle spin to 700,000 vibrations per mono-second triggers the initial acceleration of our physiological circuitry. As we stabilize this new vibration the resonance of light in the main power current of our spinal column increases and our physical body feels lighter.

At 800,000, we synergize our resonance of light within the first 12 rays of illumination, as their color spectrum enhances our ability to perceive images through cosmic insight. We also synergize the frequencies of 12 solar gateways into our chakratic circuitry. As we amplify our electron particle spin to 900,000 vibrations per mono-second, we energetically feel the cosmic cadence of the solar heart, as our own pulsating rhythm.

At 1,000,000 vibrations we energetically feel our light, as christ-light, within the protective cocoon of the ascension flame. As we amplify our electron particle spin to 1,100,000, we shift our awareness to our physiological circuitry and experience the assimilation of a new blueprint.

At 1,200,000 vibrations per mono-second, we delve deeper into our physiological circuitry and assimilate this new blueprint into our cells. From 1,300,000 to 2,000,000 vibrations, we synergize our own resonant pulsation of light within 15 templates of subtle circuitry.

At the frequency of 2,300,000 vibrations per mono-second, we consciously embody our resonant frequency of angelic light and bring this awareness home to where we are on earth.

As we amplify our electron particle spin to 2,500,000 vibrations, we energetically synergize the interstellar blueprint or galactic lightbody, *gaweah* [gah way]. This blueprint is known as the *merkabah*: [mer-ka-bah] *mer* is light, *ka* is spirit; *ba* is body, and our resonant pulsation of light within its unified frequency enables us to transport to and from another dimension or star system.

At 2,700,000, we consciously journey in our lightbody to each of the planets in earth's star system and activate the remembrance of all that we are in these interplanetary civilizations. As we continue our lightbody journey to each of the star systems in earth's galaxy, we remember the true lineage of our intergalactic origin.

At 3,000,000 vibrations, we consciously experience our androgynous communion and energetically feel our resonant pulsation of light, as ain soph or. As we amplify our electron particle spin to 3,500,000, we embody our light within the cosmic cross, and personify its essence as it emanates from the star systems in earth's galaxy.

At 3,800,000, we radiate our light throughout infinity. As we amplify our electron particle spin to 4,000,000 vibrations per mono-second, we emanate mastery and live as conscious creators on the new earth.

The keys in this book support the continual progression and amplification of your electron particle spin. Because the vibrational frequency of each individual is different, the use of these vibrations per mono-second vary. This requires you to be flexible and use a lower or higher vibration to actually attain the designated resonant frequency of light within each key. Before you begin each key it is recommended you set an intention to receive the vibration per mono-second that is appropriate for you. Continue using a key until you energetically feel its specified frequency.

Vesica Piscis and the Electron Particle Spin

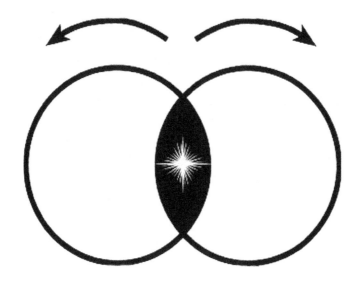

Key: Accelerate Your Electron Particle Spin

Begin the acceleration of your electron particle spin through the use of the sacred symbol, the vesica piscis, which consists of 2 overlapping energetic discs of light. This acceleration occurs as you energetically feel different waves of energy flow through the main power current of your spinal column.

Observe the accompanying illustration before you begin to energetically feel this momentum.

✿   ✿   ✿

Place your awareness in the center of the solar heart, and feel its cosmic cadence as your pulsating rhythm.... Shift your awareness to the main power current in your spinal column.... Breathe into this central meridian, and energetically feel the pulsation of your light flow with the momentum of your breath....

Intuitively sense your light in the center of the sacred symbol, vesica piscis.... Place this symbol at your coccyx/sacrum, the base of the main power current in your spinal column.... Set the intention to energetically feel the spinning momentum of its 2 overlapping discs of light....

Sense the vibration of these discs at your sacrum, and through your intention, spin them at a minimum of 100,000 vibrations.... Take a deep breath.... As these discs spin in their natural direction, feel the pulsating acceleration in the main power current of your spinal column....

Energetically feel your own resonant pulsation of gold-platinum light in the center of the vesica piscis, and amplify your electron particle spin towards 200,000 vibrations per mono-second.... Bring this pulsation of light upward through the main power current, and feel it accelerate throughout your spinal column....

In this moment, be fully present with your experience.... Shift your awareness to the center of the earth-star, and feel your light within it.... Energetically feel the resonant frequency of your electron particle spin and ground it into your physiological circuitry....

When ready, bring your awareness to where you are in the moment, and breathe into your experience.

✪   ✪   ✪

Streams of consciousness
flow in and out of inclusion,
as our breath flows in and out
of the cosmic stream.

Earth: University of Experience

Completion of Soul Contracts

Unified consciousness is the breath of first creation, which descends as soul, and the breath of soul is our consciousness in human embodiment.

The completion of soul contracts takes lifetimes of learning, yet is only a moment's experience in the vastness of the spiritual curriculum of multidimensional life. As a result, the spiritual principles that reign throughout this unified time-space continuum are unlike the human laws that govern 3rd dimensional reality.

Soul directs each lifestream towards the fulfillment of its contracts according to its divine blueprint. To attain this, soul, as an evolving spark of light, dons its garment of human embodiment for experience with other souls.

Consider that this universe functions as a spiritual university and earth is one of the divisions that house many schools as part of its university of experience. Each school is a hologram where souls rendezvous and complete contracts with other souls. In these earth-based holograms, soul places essential tests in our physical reality in the perfect time and place. As we experience these tasks or challenges they often create inner discomfort, appear as obstacles, and yet indicate profound growth. Therefore, obstacles actually assist us in understanding the meaning of life, the purpose for our connection with one another and facilitate us as we attain enlightenment. While you are on earth, are you willing to attend to the essential clearing that is required for the completion of your contracts?

Earth's university of experience is recorded as a complex etheric form of energetic tapestry with intricately woven threads of consciousness. This tapestry sustains the primary curriculum that magnetically attracts us to one another. Soul contracts, prearranged before embodiment, take many forms, some of which are short-term and others bridge lifetimes of incarnation. These spiritual contracts are the key to our participation on earth and facilitate in the synthesis of residual energetic threads in our consciousness. Rather than perceive 2 or more souls as clashing during the completion of various contracts, it is beneficial that we redefine any interaction as an opportunity for completion. These interactions are always divinely guided, and if we pay attention to our inner direction, we experience profound changes from within. Therefore, it is essential that we express gratitude and welcome the momentum of this flow.

Soulmate contracts either create experiences of joy, or they facilitate emotional triggers to unresolved memories; therefore, they mirror that which we need to see within ourselves. Through these contracts we experience reflections of our consciousness as they play out in relationships with family, friends, business partners, intimate relationships, and so on. Each soul contract offers us a spiritual gift that transfigures our perception into a heightened peak of awareness. If soul contracts remain incomplete, due to unrecognized needs and egoic desires, the opportunity to experience the spiral of authentic joy and inner freedom is lost.

As we experience the momentum of the quantum shift, it is vital that we take full responsibility for the cycles that reinforce the repetition of unresolved contracts, complete all prearranged agreements and consciously graduate from earth's university of experience.

On the new earth all soul contracts are based upon heartfelt connections, which support us at the spiritual and emotional levels. These connections clear the way for balanced stable relationships and facilitate the potential experience of profound intimacy with the beloved complement, discussed later in this book.

In support of your inner communion, it is crucial that you energetically feel your own resonant pulsation of light as you connect with other souls.

Key: Experience Soul Connection

This key is a preliminary exercise that enables you to energetically feel the presence of soul. It is also an opportunity for you to determine whether it is appropriate for you to merge your soul energy with another lifestream's, and bond at the heart level. There are 2 parts to this key, which require that each partner stand and face each other. When appropriate, use this key with a special friend or your intimate partner.

✿   ✿   ✿

Begin by looking at each other through both eyes, and then shift your focus to the left eye, the eye of soul. While using this exercise, maintain your focus and remain present with any morphing that occurs in the face of your partner.

Providing both of you are comfortable with the visual and energetic changes that occur, proceed with the following exercise.

✿

Stand face-to-face with one another, and if comfortable, join hands.... Shift your focus to each other's eyes, and maintain eye contact through most of this exercise.... Intuitively sense an energetic connection between you, and breathe into your experience....

Shift your visual focus from both eyes to the left eye.... Through your intention, emanate the color blue to your partner, and as it penetrates both your heart centers, intuitively sense a greater depth to the connection between you.... As this frequency flows through both of you, embrace each other with a heart-to-heart hug.... Sustain the hug, and energetically feel the sensation of heat as it permeates your heart centers....

Begin humming in a low tone.... Hum slightly louder, and allow the hums to synchronize as one tone.... Intuitively sense the energetic fusion between your auras, and feel your own resonant pulsation of blue light emanate from each of you.... Feel the union of this soul connection, as its pulse vibrates throughout both of your circuit systems.... Energetically feel your light spin your electron particles at a minimum of 200,000 vibrations per mono-second.... Take another deep breath, and be fully present with your experience....

When ready, disconnect from your hug, yet maintain your connection through full eye contact.... Slowly step back from each other, close your eyes, and remain in a place of gratitude for your experience....

Shift your awareness to the center of the earth-star, and feel your light within it.... Energetically feel your own resonance of light as it grounds into your physiological circuitry....

When ready, bring your awareness to where you are in the moment, and breathe into your experience.

✿　✿　✿

Neutrality Within Polarization

Earth is a planet that reinforces the hologram of duality and polarization. This hologram assists us in our conscious understanding of polarization and triggers an energetic interaction, which pulls us towards a dualistic perception that magnetically attracts what is familiar, yet remains unrecognized.

As we experience the momentum of the quantum shift light continues to magnetically attract the dark so that we transmute unconscious issues that surface for resolution. Some of the most subtle unrecognized polarities are that of spirituality or materialism, light or dark, and known or unknown. In the new matrix of life this magnetism is non-existent, as all separation unifies.

If we are trapped in other polarized language; such as, the basic examples of true and false, good and bad, thought and emotion, independent and dependent, and so on, perception of the balance point is inaccessible; therefore, we subconsciously reinforce the polarity between belief or thought, which further pulls us off balance. It is essential that we bring neutrality to all beliefs and thoughts that require an active release. For example, some of us believe we are very spiritual when it comes to the acceptance of our divinity, yet if we reinforce any form of external reference through thought or language, we are trapped in polarization. It is like being on either end of a seesaw—the momentum of the opposite polarities create imbalance, whereas the neutral point emanates balance. Yet, it is through our imbalanced perception that we focus attention on these dualistic polarities, which in truth are incompatible with the new matrix of life. Therefore, neutrality within polarization requires the personal commitment to energetically defuse the language that creates it.

The new matrix of life requires that we energetically neutralize the frequency of one polarity and then the frequency of its opposing polarity, so that our beliefs and thoughts co-exist in harmony. We shift out of having *to become* and into a conscious *state of being*. We stand in our divine light versus unconsciously following the shadow of delusion.

Key: Neutralize Polarization in Your Consciousness

In this key you energetically neutralize cerebral resonance that create polarized language. Basic examples of polarity are: true or false, good or bad, surrender or resistance, thought or emotion, conscious or unconscious, independence or dependence, spirituality or materialism, light or dark, known or unknown, and so on. As you feel the frequency of these polarities, you energetically neutralize them so that they co-exist in harmonious action.

Allow your inner guidance to direct the pace of this key. However, if it is necessary to interrupt the flow, direct your light into the center of the earth-star, and resume with the next set of polarities when appropriate. Know that you can use this key to neutralize any other polarities that surface within your awareness.

✿   ✿   ✿

With an open mind, set the conscious intention to balance any cerebral resonance to the polarities in this key....

Focus your awareness in the center of the solar heart, and energetically feel its cosmic cadence as your pulsating rhythm.... Intuitively sense any resonance with the polarization of true or false.... Place your consciousness in the center of this polarization, and command these polarities to come into balance.... Shift your awareness to the polarization of good or bad, sense any resonance with it, and then feel these polarities shift into balance.... Intuitively sense any resonance to the polarization of surrender or resistance, and energetically bring these polarities into alignment....

Through conscious intention, project your light into the polarizations of true and false, good and bad, as well as surrender and resistance, so that their polarities co-exist in harmonious action.... When ready, proceed to the next set of polarizations....

Place your consciousness in the polarization of thought or emotion, and intuitively sense any resonance.... Through your intention, energetically align this polarity.... Shift your awareness to the polarization of conscious or unconscious, and balance any resonance with it.... Sense the polarization of independence or dependence, feel any resonance with it, and then energetically align these polarities....

Through your intention, project your light into the polarizations of thought and emotion, conscious and unconscious, as well as independence and dependence, and feel them shift into harmonious action.... Proceed to the last set of polarizations in this key....

Intuitively sense the polarization of spirituality or materialism, and bring these polarities into balance.... Shift your awareness to the polarization of light or dark, feel any resonance with it, and then command them to come into balance... Intuitively sense any resonance to the polarization of known or unknown, and align these polarities....

Through conscious intention, energetically project your light into the polarizations of spirituality and materialism, light and dark, as well as known and unknown, so that their polarities co-exist in harmonious action....Feel your own resonance of light balance other polarities within your thoughts and verbal communication....

Energetically feel your own resonant pulsation of gold-platinum light in the center of the vesica piscis, and command its 2 overlapping discs to spin your electron particles at a minimum of 200,000 vibrations per mono-second....

Amplify your electron particle spin towards 300,000 vibrations, and feel the momentum of acceleration in the main power current of your spinal column....

Shift your awareness to the center of the earth-star, and feel your light within it.... Energetically emanate neutrality and balance into your thoughts, and ground it into your physiological circuitry....

When ready, bring your awareness to where you are in the moment, and breathe into your experience.

✡   ✡   ✡

Cerebral-Emotional Circuitry

Cerebral-emotional circuitry is a complex system of bi-directional network in which each can alter the other. The cerebral part of this system has intricate circuits that respond to our intention, focus and concentration. Appropriate use of this circuitry amplifies our innate ability to master our thoughts and influence the way in which we view life. Our emotional circuitry, comprised of sentiment and the bodily sensation of sight, sound, taste, smell and touch is intricately intertwined; therefore, both systems rely upon each other in order to function in a healthy way.

The human brain is like a complex computer system that reinforces logical programs, filters and stores sensory input, as well as associates it with other events or stimuli that occur in any synapse or receptor along the way. In the cerebral circuitry of the brain all sensory information undergoes a filtering process as it travels across one or more synapses, and eventually reaches appropriate areas in the brain, like the frontal lobes, where sensory input enters our conscious awareness.

In 3rd dimensional density our degree of intelligence refers to knowledge, and since new understanding is in the forefront, the left brain is on overload as it struggles to maintain what it knows. During our momentum of the quantum shift, it is crucial that we shift our awareness from logical interaction to full conscious knowing, as resistance to this imminent alteration depletes our ability to release solidified thought patterns. The shift from left brain logical interaction to this new impetus of right brain knowing naturally enables us to use a greater percentage of our brain capacity. As we experience brain synchronicity, we neutralize the function of our cerebral circuitry and navigate new direction in day-to-day life.

In the sentiment part of this complex system emotional residue filters into our awareness from other dimensional timelines of consciousness. Due to karmic outplay from experiences in these timelines, any energetic imbalance creates cycles of repetition that manifest as emotional instability. Stabilization of our emotional circuitry transcends imbalance into a non-involved focus without attachment; therefore, we experience sentiment yet, monitor emotion from a place of observation.

As we value the way in which cerebral-emotional circuitry intertwines with our conscious awareness, we balance our resonance of light within it and experience neutrality. Let's begin with the cerebral circuitry sector of this complex system.

Belief System and Its Core Imprint

Consciousness is vast and through the law of attraction, returns to all that we are in the center of creation. Therefore, each thought interweaves throughout time and space and eventually returns to us through our own projection, which defines how we experience life.

Consider the perspective that consciousness is like the canopy of an open umbrella that filters multiple thoughts through the cerebral part of our brain. The more we allow these thoughts to encumber our belief system, the more we implant their subtle energy into our awareness. As we internalize these thoughts their external influences create fragmentation within our awareness. Unless we neutralize this dissonance as it passes through our mind, these thoughts are absent in awareness and manifest into our reality as well as in parallel realities. Are you fully present with each thought as it passes through your awareness?

Life's experiences are a direct reflection of our belief system, which is the framework for the holograms that reinforce repetition. These holograms impact our thoughts and reinforce the echo of mind activity, which affects our awareness as a whole. Usually this activity is self-imposed and creates imbalance and impeding realities in our day-to-day life. As a result, all beliefs reside in the subconscious mind; therefore, it takes action for the conscious mind to attain full resolution of the inner conditioning that governs our belief system. Psychological analysis of this process continually reinforces subliminal restriction and prevents us from attaining neutrality throughout our belief system. This action often becomes the subtle deceiver, which keeps us in a cocoon until we set ourselves free; therefore, it is crucial that we are consciously aware of how this repetition affects our day-to-day life.

As we transfigure our beliefs we deliberately use our conscious mind to shift the intellectual framework that governs them. For example, a lifestream with the imprint of rejection identifies with the thought that "no matter what I do, it is never good enough." A conscious intention that remedies this thought is:

✿   ✿   ✿

"*I AM* bathed in the light of infinite love, and
create balanced relationships with others who acknowledge me."

✿   ✿   ✿

It is crucial that we explore our beliefs more fully, tune into the core imprint that perpetuates their repetition, and reflect upon whether these beliefs serve our highest purpose. Each time we transcend limiting beliefs, the superconscious transmits through the guidance system of thought, and directs vital information through the conscious mind.

This essential information is stored in an archive known as the hall of akashic records. The matrix of its holographic data sustains a photographic plate of the universe that holds the complete soul records for the evolution of humanity. These records contain the files of our experiences within every dimension as well as within every star system, galaxy and universe.

Our personal file contains the memory of our core imprint, as well as 4 other imprints, which are offshoots of our soul level challenge. The memory of our core imprint solidifies into form as a result of our 1st individualized experience with our soul-spark. As we become aware of this imprint, we enhance our perception and neutralize repetitive beliefs and thoughts that create imbalance in our day-to-day lives. Hence, we take full responsibility for the cause of our original creation and its affect on our belief system. This is how we attain balance in our cerebral circuitry.

Since the imprints that manifest in our present reality do so for the purpose of clearing, it is essential that we transform the underlying issue. This clearing sets into motion the stream of thoughtforms that accompany our experiences from one incarnation to another, such as: abandonment, unworthiness, betrayal, inadequacy and rejection. These imprints have energetic counterparts that bring up memories from the subconscious region of our cerebral circuitry. Take a moment and contemplate the following questions: Do you accept that your life experiences are a reflection of your core imprint? Are you able to articulate your core beliefs, and if so, what beliefs limit your inner authority?

Following is a list of *I AM* intentions that assist in the transfiguration of our core imprint as well as our belief system:

Core Imprint	*I AM Intention*
Abandonment	*I AM* surrounded by infinite love.
	I AM whole and complete within myself.
	I AM at peace here on earth.
Unworthiness	*I AM* aware of my true worth.
	I AM certain of my inner knowing.
	I AM an integral part of the divine plan.
Betrayal	*I AM* forgiving of those who betray me.
	I AM in full discernment.
	I AM in the flow with all life.
Inadequacy	*I AM* capable beyond measure.
	I AM fulfilled in every moment.
	I AM in charge of my destiny.
Rejection	*I AM* bathed in the light of acceptance.
	I AM the heart of infinite love.
	I AM unified consciousness.

Key: Neutralize Your Core Imprint

Your primary core imprint follows you throughout many lifetimes and as you remember the original cause of this imprint, you neutralize the beliefs embedded as the echo of mind activity.

Neutralization of your core imprint requires that you accept responsibility for the creation of your belief system, and claim the thoughts that you originally set into motion. Use this key repeatedly for any in-depth thoughtforms that surface.

✡   ✡   ✡

Begin by sensing the unconscious beliefs that prevent you from neutralizing your core imprint.... Set the pure intention to deactivate this imprint, as well as the beliefs and thoughts that reinforce it....

Place your consciousness in the solar heart, and energetically feel its cosmic cadence as your pulsating rhythm.... Envision a sphere of light above your crown, and superimpose each belief into this sphere.... Shift your awareness to the center of this sphere of light, and place your consciousness within it.... Assimilate any additional awareness of other beliefs as they surface from the subconscious.... Stabilize these beliefs while they are in the sphere of light, and emanate your light into them to neutralize their frequency....

When ready, tune into one of your thoughts, and be fully present with it as it filters through your awareness.... Take a moment and be fully aware of any other thoughts that pass through your mind, and then listen to the echo of activity that accompany them.... Synthesize these thoughts into the cerebral sector of your brain, and neutralize their frequencies with your light....

Shift your awareness to the hall of akashic records, located in the etheric archives.... With reverence, walk up its illuminated staircase, and energetically feel your resonance of light inside this holographic archive.... Go directly to the file that holds the record of your core imprint.... Before you remove this file, invoke divine right action and energetically imprint its location into your conscious memory....

Open this file, and locate the core imprint of your 1st experience of individuation.... Assimilate the remembrance that this core imprint transmits.... Intuitively sense any other imprints that require synthesis, and assimilate their

49

frequencies.... Integrate the spiritual wisdom that comes to you from these imprint(s), and bring this knowing full circle.... Shift your awareness, and return to the original location that sustains your soul records.... Replace the file of your core imprint in its correct position, and with reverence express gratitude for your remembrance by declaring the following spoken word:

> "The core imprint in my belief system neutralizes, and
> all thoughtforms shift into balance.
> *I AM* free."

Feel your light spin your electron particles at a minimum of 300,000 vibrations per mono-second.... Energetically feel your resonant pulsation of gold-platinum light in the center of the vesica piscis, and command its 2 overlapping discs to spin.... Amplify your electron particle spin towards 400,000 vibrations per mono-second....

Feel your resonance of light neutralize your core imprint, and be aware of all sensations in your physical body.... With gratitude, exit the hall of akashic records, and walk down the illuminated staircase....

Shift your awareness to the center of the earth-star, and feel your light within it.... Energetically feel your light create a new matrix of beliefs and thoughts, and then implant them into your cerebral circuitry....

When ready, bring your awareness to where you are in the moment, and breathe into your experience.

✡　✡　✡

Neutrality in Emotional Circuitry

Human life is filled with repetitive emotional cycles that occur without the conscious awareness of their true purpose. Emotions are directly related to what we believe about ourselves and how strongly we maintain these beliefs; therefore, they are based in the subconscious and have direct knowing of how to attract like frequencies.

Feelings of sentiment accompany emotions, which are often obscured by fictions of the mind. These sensations create the essential unfolding activity of transformation; therefore, the primary currents of this energetic momentum are the juice of life. For that reason, it is crucial that we befriend our own body and enter into the mysteries of the flesh, in order to approach our inner emotional work with enthusiasm and curiosity.

Emotion is energy-in-motion, and naturally flows throughout the physical body as an instantaneous thrust of movement. As emotions surface they act as transmitters that decode molecular and cellular knowing. These transmitters ignite the frequency of fire and water throughout our cells and shift both elements into an energetic current that flows throughout our circuitry. Because emotions build upon their own momentum, if imbalanced, the lack of inner movement creates energetic debris that crystallizes in the physical body. Although the cause of this debris differs due to individual experience, it reinforces residual feelings, which create non-cognitive information that dominates our state of awareness and causes energetic cords of attachment to form throughout the circuit system.

Excessive emotional dissonance causes fragmentation throughout our psyche, feelings of discord in our emotions and energetic chaos within our cells. This occurs as the emotional charge passes through our physiological circuitry. As we feel the energetic current of each charge, we experience the perfect moment to assimilate its pulsation and decode essential wisdom relevant to our attainment of inner balance. Each energetic current is a profound source of spiritual nourishment that ignites inner freedom.

Thought + feeling = emotion
Emotion = energy-in-motion
Energy-in-motion = teacher within

Unfortunately, most lifestreams resist identifying the underlying causes behind their emotional issues and seek material solutions to their experiences. Although this often creates discomfort, pain and disease in our physical body, these underlying emotional challenges are a perfect opportunity for self-reflection.

As we experience the momentum of the quantum shift, our transmutation of imbalanced emotions depends on our acceptance for what is occurring in the moment. It feels as if we are falling into a black hole, yet the basis from which we bring our emotions to their neutral point is through reconciliation. As we center our awareness in the core of each emotion, all energetic charges flow directly through or around us without attaching anywhere in our circuit system. Emotional harmony stabilizes any arising conditions, synergizes all attachment and creates inner freedom; therefore, we consciously experience sentiment as deeper states of awareness.

In the new matrix of life emotional health prevails and demands that we become conscious of the unconscious.

Key: Neutralize Your Emotions

As you energetically neutralize your emotions, be aware of the wisdom that surfaces from within and observe how your body presents this information to you.

✡   ✡   ✡

Focus your awareness in the center of the solar heart, and energetically feel its cosmic cadence as your pulsating rhythm.... Envision the presence of your angelic self behind you, and set the intention to neutralize your emotions....

Remember one emotional issue that you would like to neutralize.... When you energetically feel the presence of this emotion, envision the issue on a piece of parchment paper.... Roll the paper into a scroll, tie it with a colored ribbon of your choice, and place this scroll on one of your shoulders....

Be aware of your angelic presence behind you, and as this resonance of light, wrap your angel wings around your physical body.... Feel your angelic presence lift the scroll from your shoulder.... Take a deep breath, and with absolute certainty, give permission to this angelic part of yourself to return this energy to its original point of creation.... When ready, be aware of any other emotion that surfaces, and breathe into the feelings that arise within you.... Feel your own resonant pulsation of infinite love as your angelic essence fades from your sight for the present moment....

Energetically feel your resonant pulsation of gold-platinum light spin your electron particles at a minimum of 400,000 vibrations per mono-second... Through the conscious intention to neutralize your emotions, declare the following spoken word:

> "You have a right to be here and there,
> As you reveal your emotions to me.
> With gratitude, thank you,
> for now is the time to realign your energy
> on the altar of infinite love, and
> return to the source of your original point of creation.
> And so it is. It is done."

In this moment feel the release of this emotional energy.... Shift your awareness to the center of the earth-star, and feel your light within it.... Energetically feel your light as it grounds a new frequency into your physiological circuitry....

When ready, bring your awareness to where you are in the moment, and be fully present with your experience.

✿   ✿   ✿

Memory Within Cellular Circuitry

Cellular memory has an intelligence of its own that lies dormant in the nuclei of the cells. The seed of this intelligence is stored as spiritual knowing in the medulla oblongata, at the base of the brain. If we resist the causes and conditions that we set into motion, spiritual knowing remains locked in the medulla and cellular memory is blocked in the chromosomes of our cells.

As cellular memory rises to the surface, its current carries a momentum of energetic eruption that is disruptive to our emotional world. The momentum of this energetic current takes many forms, including kinetic sensations, electrical charges, burning, chills, tingling, twitching, and so on. As this current sweeps through us, waves of energy ripple throughout our physiological circuitry. This energetic momentum sustains the essence of our knowing; therefore, the depth of natural restoration depends on our complete acceptance of what is occurring in the moment. The instant that an energetic current leaves the cell, we energetically feel the *eye of the storm* as it releases residual memory from our physiological circuitry.

The release of cellular memory unifies both light (forward momentum) and dark (stagnation), and fuses separation in our consciousness. It accelerates the frequency of light in our cells and prepares the groundwork for us to assimilate residue within our threads of consciousness.

Key: Neutralize Cellular Memory

In this key you energetically neutralize cellular memory as it emerges from the nuclei of your cells. Each time you experience this key, you transmute causes and conditions that you originally set into motion, so be patient as your physical body attains another threshold of freedom and wholeness.

✿ ✿ ✿

Place your consciousness in the center of the solar heart and energetically feel its cosmic cadence as your pulsating rhythm.... Set the intention to neutralize memory within your cells, as it surfaces from deep within your circuitry....

Shift your awareness to the cellular circuitry in your physical body, and intuitively sense your frequency in the nucleus of one of your cells.... Delve deeper into this circuitry, and while in the depth of your own awareness, shift to the nucleus of another cell, and be aware of the sensations that occur in your body.... Intuitively sense your light in the nuclei of other cells, and as it infuses with their knowing, lovingly assimilate the awareness that surfaces....

Fill the nuclei of your cells with gold-platinum light, and emanate this radiance throughout your circuitry.... Be aware of all other energetic sensations that arise in your physical body, and remain fully present with your experience....

Energetically feel your own resonant pulsation of this light spin your electron particles at a minimum of 400,000 vibrations per mono-second.... Through conscious intention and with absolute certainty, declare the following spoken word:

"The chromosomes in the nuclei of my cells
assimilate enlightenment.
Full conscious knowing within my cells is at hand."

Shift your awareness to the center of the earth-star, and feel your light within it....
Energetically feel the sensation of enlightenment in the nuclei of your cells, as it
grounds full knowing into your cellular circuitry....

When ready, bring your awareness to where you are in the moment, and breathe
into your experience.

✿   ✿   ✿

Timelines of Consciousness

Consciousness flows in and out of inclusion, just as our breath flows in and out of
the cosmic stream. It weaves its essence as a grid of light that crisscrosses over
and under all timelines of our evolutionary journey.

Timelines of consciousness co-exist side-by-side within the tapestry of life, yet
extend throughout infinity, where we integrate aspects of our own familiarity
from wherever we are in any given moment. However, until we balance our
awareness in the material world and accept that other timelines are real, they
appear non-existent.

Our conscious understanding of the diversity in these timelines depends on
our ability to remember in accordance with our own timing. Although
experiences in other dimensions are somewhat altered to that which occurs in 3rd
dimensional reality their energetic patterns are genuine. These timelines emanate
their threads of awareness as present-day experiences, yet play out similar
scenarios in parallel or alternate realities. These realities are a direct result of the
energetic fusion of our consciousness, which often makes it challenging to
determine which dimensional timeline we are living in; therefore, we manifest
similar experiences in day-to-day life.

As all timelines merge we participate in multiple realities through simultaneous lifetimes in parallel dimensions. This awareness reinforces the theory that multiplicities in time and space exist as one time-space continuum.

Threads of Consciousness

Threads of consciousness comprise an energetic web of tapestry that projects cords of attachment. These cords recycle subtle energy patterns from one incarnation to another; therefore, if the cause of attachment is left unresolved we perpetually experience cycles of repetition in our day-to-day life.

As we acknowledge these cycles, we become aware of one or more residual energetic cords, and where appropriate, reconcile with the remembrance of experiences attached to these cords. The more we neutralize these memories, the more we naturally synthesize threads of consciousness from the past and bring this awareness into the present moment. In doing so, we move through experiences that play out in several realities at the same time.

Are you consciously aware of the experiences that reinforce your own cords of attachments? How many times do you say, "I thought I was finished with this issue," yet you repeat the same experience again and again?

With absolute certainty, declare the following spoken word:

✿   ✿   ✿

"I AM the past and the present.
Reconciliation of the past
releases all but that, which serves me.
All that is in the palm of my hand
is the present moment."

✿   ✿   ✿

Key: Assimilate Your Threads of Consciousness

In this key you intuitively sense the frequency of timeline(s) that sustain your own energetic threads of consciousness. These threads have multiple cords of attachment, which on an energy level affect your cerebral-emotional circuitry. Assimilation of these threads requires that you neutralize their cords of attachment so that the past is reconciled into the present moment. It is essential that you energetically feel your own resonant pulsation of light within these cords and accept the transmission of essential information as it surfaces. Repeat this key as often as is necessary for assimilation of threads in the 3rd dimensional timeline, as well as threads within other dimensions.

✿ ✿ ✿

Create a comfortable space in your environment.... Focus your awareness in the center of the solar heart, and energetically feel its cosmic cadence as your pulsating rhythm.... Invoke divine right action as you enter the depth of your own awareness....

Shift your awareness to the intricate web of tapestry that intertwines with your consciousness.... Intuitively sense your resonance of light within this web as it crisscrosses over, under and through *this* earth timeline.... Place your consciousness in a sphere of cobalt blue light, and intuitively sense your resonance of light in its frequency.... Sense if there are any cords of attachment that project from the energetic threads in *this* timeline, and be aware of any sensations in your physical body....

Through conscious intention, focus your awareness on one of these threads, and sense the cords of attachment that project from it.... Fill these cords with your light, and assimilate it into this thread....

Shift your awareness to another thread of consciousness, and intuitively sense its cords of attachment.... Fill these cords with your light, and synthesize it within this thread.... When ready, shift your consciousness to any other threads that appear in your awareness, and intuitively sense the frequency of their cords.... Fill these cords with your light, and see them assimilate into their threads....

Feel your resonance of light spin your electron particles at a minimum of 400,000 vibrations per mono-second, and be fully present with any sensations in your body.... Through your intention, declare the following spoken word:

> *"I AM* a neutral observer, and
> place all threads of consciousness
> in the present moment.
> *I AM* free, and
> synergize neutrality within all timelines."

Energetically feel your own resonant pulsation of gold-platinum light in the center of the vesica piscis, and command its 2 overlapping discs to spin.... Amplify your electron particle spin towards 500,000 vibrations, and feel this accelerated frequency in the main power current of your spinal column....

Shift your awareness to the center of the earth-star, and feel your light within it.... Energetically feel your own resonance of cobalt-blue light, as it grounds into your circuit system....

When ready, bring your awareness to where you are in the moment, and breathe into your experience.

✿   ✿   ✿

Multidimensional Timelines

The cosmic laws that reign throughout multidimensional timelines are unlike the physical laws that dominate the 3rd dimension. All dimensions of time and space emanate as a unified continuum therefore, it is essential that we transfigure material density to a cohesive state of awareness.

Webster's dictionary defines the word *dimension* as "a magnitude measured in a particular direction," which determines the "location of an object or event in time and space." In our attempt to comprehend the multidimensional timelines that our consciousness weaves through, it is essential that we understand the difference between how dimensional space functions. One-dimensional space is a single line, 2-dimensional space is flat, 3-dimensional space has length, width and height, and 4-dimensional space synergizes space and time.

A more advanced explanation on the concept of *dimension* is a limitless range of frequencies in which everything exists simultaneously; therefore, a dimension is another state of existence that reflects; as above, is below. Although the primary focus of this book is conscious ascension into the matrix of the 5th dimension, it stretches our awareness to energetically feel the multidimensional frequencies between the 5th and the 9th dimensions. Some lifestreams on earth are aware that there are 24 known dimensions, yet there are an infinite number of dimensions within other dimensions that intertwine with our consciousness on a subtle level. If we are unawakened to these non-ordinary realities, we have yet to energetically experience our own multidimensional expansion. If we desire to live life to our full human potential, it is essential that we energetically feel our own pulsation of light within these multidimensional timelines, for it is our light that leads us to attain self-actualization and conscious mastery.

Frequencies of the first 12 dimensions intertwine with the 3rd dimension through our consciousness. During the momentum of our conscious ascension, we are able to energetically feel their frequencies as they interpenetrate one another and subtly weave through our awareness. In actuality everything exists simultaneously; therefore, our consciousness always shifts in and out of these dimensions as well as throughout the 12 octaves of light in each dimension. Are you open to the perspective that your consciousness shifts in and out of an infinite number of dimensions?

The following information is a general overview of the first 12 dimensions, 3 of which are earth-based and 9 that are of etheric substance. As you read through this overview, pay attention to the way in which your body responds to these multidimensional timelines of consciousness.

1st Dimension—mineral world. Consciousness within this dimension has the slowest vibratory rate on earth, yet it sustains information on the creation of earth;

2nd Dimension—kingdom of nature and the world of devas and fairies. The stellar frequency within this kingdom sustains a grid of light that supports human intelligence;

3rd Dimension—supports our life force on earth as we experience physicality and linear time. This dimension is a material plane of existence, where we humans incarnate to consciously experience all that we are, as god. While in this dimension, we have the opportunity to transmute all dissonance within our awareness and fully embody our light on earth;

4th Dimension—the frequency of this dimension intertwines with our consciousness in the intergalactic civilization of anunnaki, on planet nibiru. It is a corridor of time and space through which our resonance of light in the polarized realm of archetypal forces interacts with our consciousness while we are on earth. As the frequency of this dimension intertwines with our day-to-day life, it neutralizes our cerebral-emotional circuitry, and activates feelings as well as expressions that lie dormant in the human heart. Its frequency overlaps 3rd dimensional reality and instills the desire for unity and peace. As we attain a greater sense of union this polarized realm merges with its new resonance of light and self-imposed separation in consciousness synergizes;

5th Dimension—sustains encodements that are invisible to the human eye, yet it is the gateway to the matrix of multidimensional life. The frequency of this dimension intertwines with our resonance of light in the intergalactic civilizations of the star system pleiades. It supports the knowing that everything is always in divine order and for the highest good of all concerned. In this dimension spirituality is an inner authority that emerges as our living reality; therefore we live in equality, balance, harmony, synchronicity and conscious mastery in day-to-day life. As we experience the vastness of infinity, we energetically feel our resonance of light within several dimensions on the new earth;

6th Dimension—is the lightbody form of the 3rd dimensional world. This dimension facilitates intention, focus and concentration so that we fully assimilate its geometric encodements of light. As our consciousness weaves in and out of this dimension, it transmits geometric codes from the language of light into our awareness, and energetically transfers the remembrance of human experience to the akashic records. This dimension intertwines with our consciousness in the intergalactic civilizations of the star system sirius;

7th Dimension—sustains light that emanates balance between vertical and horizontal frequencies of light. Our consciousness within this dimension intertwines with the intergalactic civilizations of the andromeda galaxy. It transmits thought, color and sound, through which tones and overtones activate another stargate that leads us to synergize awareness within other interplanetary civilizations. As our consciousness shifts in and out of this dimension, we experience the sensation of timelessness;

8th Dimension—our consciousness within this dimension assimilates the structural organization of cosmic intelligence, known as the intergalactic federation. As we weave our light within and throughout this dimension, we are consciously aware that we work in unity as group souls in support of our cosmic mission. The frequency of this dimension intertwines with our consciousness in the intergalactic civilizations of the constellation orion;

9th Dimension—intertwines with subtle frequencies in the galactic core and emanates through our resonance of light as the consciousness, enochians. It transmits geometric encodements within the language of light and assimilates them into our awareness as full conscious knowing. This dimension facilitates our assimilation of the interstellar frequency of the galactic lightbody and supports us as we anchor it into our circuit system;

10th Dimension—is where we simultaneously experience the nothing and the everything. It emanates the unified frequency of the 1 and the 0 and supports understanding of the sum being greater than its parts. This dimension assists us as we experience divinity;

11th Dimension—requires the assimilation of 2 distinct frequencies: the androgynous masculine principle of yhvh and the androgynous feminine principle of shekinah, as the unified frequency of yhsvh;

12th Dimension—an endless emanation of light that synergizes all 12 dimensions into the totality of all-that-is, where everything is equal to the whole;

13th Dimension—all time, all space, all consciousness, all knowing, unifies as one. As unified consciousness, we energetically feel our own resonant pulsation of light within an infinite number of dimensions.

Octaves of Light Within the Dimensions

Within the dimensions there are 13 octaves of light. Each octave maintains sound and brain wave frequencies, as well as planetary harmonics, and serves as an energetic conduit to its corresponding dimension. For example, much of our consciousness resides in the 3rd octave of light, yet continuously weaves in and out of the other octaves of light.

In the 3rd dimension octaves 1 - 3 - 5 emanate as frequencies throughout our physiological circuitry, and octaves 2 - 4 - 6 through 12 emanate as frequencies throughout the etheric realm. These 12 octaves of light synergize as the 13th octave and this infusion facilitates the completion of life on earth as we know it.

As our consciousness randomly weaves in and out of these octaves of light, we prepare for life in a multidimensional realm of awareness, which is paramount to our being fully present in the new matrix of life.

The following information is an overview of the frequencies for earth's 12 octaves of light, which synergize as the 13th octave on the new earth:

1st Octave—this octave of light emanates the frequencies of the mineral world into our consciousness;

2nd Octave—devas and fairies transmit frequencies of light through the kingdom of nature;

3ʳᵈ Octave—university of experience where we complete our soul contracts and synthesize our own resonance of light throughout timelines of consciousness;

4ᵗʰ Octave—polarized realm of archetypal forces;

5ᵗʰ Octave—this octave of light emanates equality, balance, harmony, synchronicity and conscious mastery, and grounds this unified frequency into our physiological circuitry;

6ᵗʰ Octave—transmits multidimensional light through geometric encodements such as blueprints, templates, grids of light, crop circles, mandalas, platonic solids and star codes;

7ᵗʰ Octave—synergizes the resonant pulsation of christ-light within the spleen; a simultaneous flow of vertical and horizontal energy;

8ᵗʰ Octave—sustains the frequency of light required for conscious creation;

9ᵗʰ Octave—grid of light that synergizes our resonance of multidimensional frequencies into our circuit system;

10ᵗʰ Octave—fusion of the 1—unity and the 0—neutrality, as a simultaneous experience of the nothing and the everything. As we weave within and throughout this octave of light, we experience conscious divinity;

11ᵗʰ Octave—is where we consciously experience our androgynous communion, as yhsvh;

12th Octave—we experience our own resonance of unified consciousness in our day-to-day life; sustains our resonance of light in the interstellar symbol of the cosmic cross;

13th Octave—synergizes our multidimensional frequency on the new earth.

The full spectrum of light in this galaxy
emanates a creative force of cosmic synergy that
flows through us in diverse ways,
supports us in numerous ways,
yet transfigures us in all ways.

Matrix of Geometric Encodements of Light

Universal Language of Light

Everything in this universe, as well as other universes, resonates to light, which transmits waves of encoded frequencies throughout all star systems and galaxies in these universes. The full spectrum of light is encoded in the blueprint of divinity and is the primary form of spiritual communication throughout consciousness.

The language of light, in all its forms, is a super holographic image that transmits different waves of frequencies, such as: sound, the spoken word, sacred tongues and sacred geometry. The latter includes images of geometric designs, star codes, platonic solids and crop circles. These images sustain advanced frequencies of cosmic intelligence that circumvent the cognitive mind, and bring forth new understanding and purpose in our lives.

Harmonics of Sound

Sound harmonizes specific frequencies that open energetic gateways within our circuit system; therefore, sound is one of the modalities that transfigure matter and energy. Every sound is distinctive as its tones and overtones pulsate throughout the cosmos, as well as permeate our awareness. Together, tones and overtones are equivalent to the resonance of creation and sustain low or high-pitched frequencies that transfigure matter into new patterns of energy.

Each time our hearing harmonizes to mono, dual, triple or quadruple tones and overtones, inner guidance prompts us to answer the celestial call, and energetically tune into the resonant pulsation of cosmic harmony that accompany these tones. As this continues to occur, it is imperative that we listen to the pitch of these tone(s), and welcome the inner knowing that it offers in that moment.

In addition to the auditory system, sound also emanates through tonal signature; therefore, from one incarnation to another, the sound of our resonant pulsation of harmonics emanates the same tone. This voice pulsation alters matter and energy through different harmonics, which transfigures the vibrational frequency to which the toning is directed. The momentum for voice toning begins in the solar plexus, and when the tone is ready to sound, the pulsation moves upward from a neutral point in the center of the chest and emanates through the throat via the movement of breath. The thoracic cage reverberates like a drum and our cells vibrate in unison with the tone. If you are interested in learning how to sound through tones and overtones, ask inner guidance to assist you.

In addition, you can choose to support earth as it attains balance with its new harmonic resonance. To begin, sound a tone to the musical note of high "f" (octave above middle "c"). The correct "f" tone can be found by ascending the musical scale beginning with middle "c," and proceeding through d, e, f, g, a, b, c, d, e, f.

The "f" tone can be sounded through voice, a musical instrument, a tuning fork or electronically. It is the resonance of sound that fuses the human heart with the cosmic cadence of the solar heart. When we sound this tone repeatedly, we amplify our light and unlock the portal to another threshold of cosmic tones and overtones from other interplanetary civilizations.

Transmissions Through the Spoken Word

In our day-to-day communication with others, we use the words "I am" without conscious awareness for the effect of its energetic impact on our framework of consciousness.

The spoken word *I AM* is a universal covenant for the innate presence as god and emanates as our own resonant pulsation of light. Its covenant serves as an stargate for our ultimate phase of ascension; therefore, it sustains the etheric threshold to the gateway that bridges all separation between human consciousness, christed-oversoul and all-that-is. The word, "*I*" is the witnessing presence of all-that-is, and the word "*AM*" is all-that-is witnessing itself.

Conscious use of the spoken word *I AM*, through invocation or decrees, sustains the highest vibrational frequency of light in earth's dimension. As we energetically feel our own resonant pulsation of light in this covenant of light, we experience self-actualization, divinity and sovereignty.

Key: Experience Your Resonant Pulsaton of the Spoken Word

In this key you energetically feel your own resonant pulsation of the spoken word *I AM*, and emanate this covenant of light through your breath.

✿   ✿   ✿

Place your consciousness in the center of the solar heart, and energetically feel its cosmic cadence as your pulsating rhythm.... As the light of *I AM*, inhale the spirit of "*I*".... As the essence of all-that-is, exhale the embodiment of "*AM*," and be fully present with all that you are, as god....

> Inhale *I*.... Exhale *AM*....
> Inhale *I*.... Exhale *AM*....
> Inhale *I*.... Exhale *AM*....

Through conscious intention and with absolute certainty, declare the following spoken word:

> "As the covenant of light
> *I AM* that *I AM*."

Energetically feel your own resonant pulsation of gold-platinum light spin your electron particles at a minimum of 500,000 vibrations per mono-second.... Emanate your light throughout the main power current of your spinal column, and feel your own essence, as all-that-is....

Shift your awareness to the center of the earth-star, and feel your light within it.... Energetically feel your covenant of light, and ground it into your physiological circuitry....

When ready, bring your awareness to where you are in the moment, and breathe into your experience.

✡   ✡   ✡

Voice of Sacred Tongues

Every earth language, in its spoken and written form, has its base in one or more sacred tongues. These tongues originate from the sacred seeds of divinity, and their resonant frequency unites many spiritual traditions practiced on earth. Each tongue emanates a specific frequency, yet together they comprise the whole.

Atlanteans speak the vril tongue, which consists of clicks and tones. The word vril means *chi* or primal life force, and is the original foundation for the tongue of the enochians, the language of the archangels. The 72 tonal signatures of this sacred tongue are derived from a single monochord, yet this number correlates to the sacred dialects for the 72 names of god.

Sanskrit, which originates from sumatran, is the tongue of the vedas, and its vedic frequency is the sacred text of hinduism. Both sanskrit and tibetan transmit vertical alignments into the circuit system. The chinese tongue and egyptian pictographic symbols transmit horizontal alignments into the circuit system.

The adamic tongue is the proto-language of earth. Remnants of this tongue are still in the hebrew language, as in yhsvh, *elohim* [e-lo-heem'], *el shaddai* [el sha-dye'], yhvh and shekinah. This ancient tongue also fragments into the tonal signatures of 72 dialects, so that our consciousness receives the frequency of the 72 names of god.

In the hebrew language traditional terms consist of consonants only. Vowel sounds are added to facilitate the pronunciation of the spoken word and the assimilation of its appropriate frequency. In its written form, the hebrew language contains 34 yods, which are fire letters with geometric codes that emanate unified frequencies of light. The original hebrew alphabet consists of 22 letters, which are:

A B G D H V Z Ch T Y K L M N S O P Tz Q R Sh Th
Aleph, Bet, Gimmel, Dalet, Hey, Vav, Zayin, Chet, Tet, Yod, Kaph, Lamed,
Mem, Nun, Samekh, Ayin, Pey, Tzaddi, Quf, Reysh, Shin and Tav.

As we consciously accept the holiness of each sacred tongue, we naturally synthesize the frequency of their spoken word and energetically feel their tonal vibrations. The more we resonate with these tones, the more we fully comprehend that our own resonant pulsation of light is being aligned to the frequency of the 5th dimension and beyond.

Language of Intergalactic Tongues

Intergalactic tongues originate from civilizations within other star systems, and these tongues transmit encodements of light that sustain cosmic intelligence. The language of these tongues filters through our consciousness and is transmitted as voice signature by the lifestream receiving the information. Understanding this language appears unattainable to the untrained mind; and it is challenging to interpret these transmissions through our intellect as it defies exact translation.

To neutralize these potential obstacles interplanetary civilizations transmit their frequencies through specific encodements of sacred geometry, and we energetically feel these codes as resonant pulsations of light. Every transmission opens a cosmic portal within us so that we energetically feel the vastness of our light and receive one or more intergalactic tongues into our awareness. To do so, it is essential that we assimilate interstellar frequencies from different star systems.

From one interplanetary citizen to another, *modem ve altruit efam*...peace.

Transmissions of Light Through Sacred Geometry

An increasingly important emanation of the language of light is sacred geometry, as its encodements energetically accelerate our frequency and visually stimulate our awareness. These codes filter through grids of light that sustain cosmic symbols and a multidimensional spectrum of colors. They transmit different frequencies through mathematical ratios, geometric proportions and shapes, which when combined in specific ways carry unique resonant qualities of light. Examples of these geometrics are found in ancient egyptian and greek temples, tibetan sand mandalas and cathedrals, as well as platonic solids, crop circles and star codes.

Crop-circles and star codes in particular emanate interstellar codes of light that deeply penetrate our awareness. As we assimilate the advanced frequency of these codes we energetically feel their energetic transmissions, as pulsations of light that flow throughout our body.

Following is a general overview of the language of light:

> **Star codes**—transmit encodements of light that emanate subtle frequencies. As we assimilate the frequencies within these codes, we receive the appropriate acceleration that is needed in a given moment to transfigure our genetic composition;

Crop circles—sophisticated mathematical formulas of complex patterns that manifest on earth in remote locations. These patterns sustain specific encodements that act as generators, which awaken codes of light within the original configuration of our dna;

Mandalas—designs that transmit cosmic intelligence through the medium of spiritual art;

Multidimensional accelerators—geometric designs with specific codes that naturally attune our consciousness to multidimensional awareness. Each design is paramount unto itself and accelerates our frequency when we allow it to energetically transfigure outdated energy patterns and thoughtforms;

Platonic solids—frequencies within the 5 platonic solids: octahedron, hexahedron, icosahedron, tetrahedron and dodecahedron facilitate our awareness of the way in which geometric blueprints continuously affect our experience of life on earth.

Without going into any scientific detail, following is a brief explanation of the way in which the frequencies of these platonic solids facilitate us as we integrate the concept of multidimensional awareness:

Hexahedron—represents the new earth, and its frequency quickens the ascension experience in each of us;

Tetrahedron—as the capstone, *shalusch* [sha loosh'], it sustains the codon of the original configuration of dna;

Icosahedron—emanates cosmic intelligence into our consciousness and supports us as we experience the momentum of our quantum shift into the new matrix of life;

Octahedron—rejuvenates and restores our circuit system through the assimilation of cosmic life force;

Icosa-dodecahedron—energetically blends water with the interstellar substance ether. This geometric air-based solid comprises pentagons and triangles into a new design that sustains advanced frequencies of light. The frequency of this geometric solid is non-material, yet real and is essential to the new matrix of life, as it naturally brings consciousness into balance so that we experience heaven and earth, simultaneously.

Regardless of where we are in our spiritual evolution, the frequency of this platonic solid assimilates into our circuit system.

Icosa-Dodecahedron

The physical body is the holy temple of the living god.

Blueprint of the 5th Dimensional Circuit System

Blueprint of the 5th Dimensional Circuit System

Ascension While in Human Embodiment

Human life represents a tiny dot, as it journeys along the spiral of light. The spiral sustains vibrational frequencies that when passed through or abided in, compress into a minute flame of light. The more we move upward on this spiral, the flame that we are expands into a larger flame. Eventually the last knowing is brought forth, the spiral is pulled inside out and the vastness of our light is fully here, where we are functioning within a physical body.

In the new matrix of life we re-create our way of living, in accordance with our understandings of the interaction of time and timelessness. We assimilate frequencies that sustain matrices of advanced energetic technologies, which restructure matter and transfigure energy in our physical body. *Sound + vibration + frequency = the power to rearrange atoms into molecules, and group the molecules into new forms of matter.*

The advanced frequencies of light within this chapter activate dormant circuits in our body and synergize the new blueprint into our circuit system. As you facilitate your own ascension experience, it is recommended that you internalize each section as addressing you personally. Are you ready to assimilate the frequency of your new blueprint into your circuit system?

Through your intention, declare the following spoken word:

✿   ✿   ✿

"*I AM* the inner flame on the spiral of light.
All limitation lifts, and *I AM* free,
merging at last, for all eternity.
I AM the spiral of light,
in human embodiment."

✿   ✿   ✿

Spiritual Dispensation of the Violet Flame

The full rainbow spectrum of light sustains frequencies that radiate luminescent colors. One of these frequencies is the violet flame, which manifests as part of our awareness through sacred practices of the melchizedek priesthood.

The violet flame is the sacred flame of transmutation and enables to use the energetic key that unlocks our inner temple of peace. The essential quality of this transmuting flame sustains a spiritual antidote for our imperfect creations. The more we recalibrate the imbalanced magnetics that accumulate in our circuit system, the more we energetically erase the cause, effect, record and memory of dissonance and clear etheric fragmentation from our grid. As we purify this imbalance we earn the right to energetically receive our own resonance of spiritual dispensation.

Key: Clear Your Grid with the Violet Flame

In this key you experience the violet flame as your own resonant pulsation of light. If you instruct your light with pure intention, it emanates the divine attributes of oneness, freedom, change, truth, clarity, balance and infinite love, all of which emit as knowing from the depth of your own awarness.

✿   ✿   ✿

Place your consciousness in the center of the earth-star, and energetically feel your light within it....

Envision a flame above the earth-star and infuse it with the color violet.... Place this flame at your coccyx, and spin it so that its frequency flows upward through the main power current of your spinal column, into your heart.... Shift your awareness to the center of the solar heart, and feel its cosmic cadence as your pulsating rhythm...

Energetically feel your light expand beyond 9 feet around your physical body.... Place your consciousness in the center of the violet flame, and project your resonant pulsation of this flame into and throughout your grid system....

Shift your awareness to the center of your grid, and envision 12 screens of tightly woven mesh.... See these screens at the outer most edges of your grid system, and bring them into your grid, so that they shift from front to back, left to right, right to left, top to bottom, as well as back and forth at diagonal angles from the foot to the opposite shoulder on both sides of the body.... Slide these mesh screens back and forth through your grid system to completely clear the fragmentation in this system.... Take a moment and breathe into your experience, then energetically feel your light balance this web of framework.... Through conscious intention and with absolute certainty, declare the following spoken word:

> "*I AM* the violet flame, and
> as this pulsation of light,
> energetically balance the framework
> of this grid system now."

When ready, bring your awareness out of the grid system, and shift it to the central meridian in your spinal column.... Energetically feel your light spin your electron particles at a minimum of 600,000 vibrations.... Feel the frequency of its spin accelerate throughout this main power current....

Shift your awareness to the base of your spinal column.... Energetically feel your resonant pulsation of gold-platinum light in the center of the vesica piscis, and command its 2 overlapping discs to spin.... Amplify your electron particle spin towards 700,000 vibrations per mono-second, and feel this acceleration throughout your circuit system.... In this moment, be fully present with your experience....

Shift your awareness to the center of the earth-star, and feel your light within it.... Energetically feel the violet flame as your resonance of light, and ground it into your physiological circuitry....

When ready, bring your awareness to where you are in the moment, and breathe into your experience.

✡   ✡   ✡

Matrix for the Violet Flame

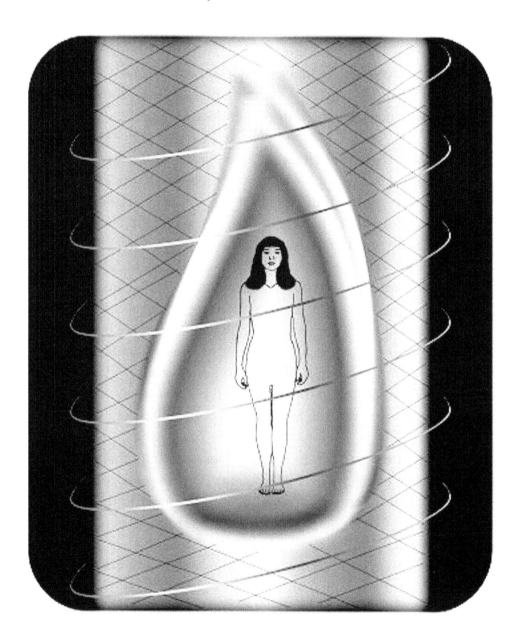

Matrix for Accelerated Physiological Circuitry

Science identifies atoms, molecules and cells as oscillating waves of light, which vibrate at varying cycles per second. Each wave of light pulsates to its own cosmic rhythm and sustains frequencies of geometric codes that energetically permeate our physiological circuitry. Assimilation of these codes synchronizes an accelerated frequency of light into our endocrine glands, organs and body systems.

Our physiological circuitry reflects an innate intelligence that is more cosmic in nature. It sustains a hologram, or a condensed elemental holding vessel, that supports the frequency of the unified circuit system. When degeneration occurs in the electrical circuitry of this hologram, its electrical charge sufficiently depletes; therefore, the physical body responds in its own way.

As we accelerate our frequency of light an energetic alignment occurs throughout our physiological circuitry, which stabilizes the mechanics of every body system and primes our body for its next phase of the ascension experience, which is assimilation of the 5th dimensional blueprint.

The following information is an overview of the endocrine glands. If you require additional awareness regarding the anatomy of your glands, or specific knowledge about the anatomy of the organs and body systems, consult available resources before you accelerate the frequency of your physiological circuitry.

Primary endocrine glands—pituitary, pineal and hypothalamus. The pituitary gland is the size of a pea, has 3 lobes and conjoins the hypothalamus. It is centrally located behind the eyes, in the center of the brain. As the master gland, the hormones it releases control all the glands except the parathyroid.

The pineal gland is pinecone-shaped, located in the middle of the brain, behind and above the pituitary. This gland affects the circadian and bio-rhythms, which influence the intertwined systems in your body. Along with the pituitary it creates vital transformation, assimilates divine will into your awareness and synchronizes cosmic cycles throughout your circuit system.

The hypothalamus is located in the lower central part of the brain, stimulates the release of hormones in the pituitary and transfigures the course of aging. Its accelerated physiological circuitry is the energetic gateway through which conscious knowing emerges;

Thymus—is under the sternum, approximately 1 inch below the notch in the center of the clavicle. It produces and releases t-cells, which fortify your immune system and energize your body;

Lymph nodes—are along the carotid arteries, in the armpits, along each side of the sternum, in the groin, at each elbow and down the sides of the legs. They filter and purify the lymph, and produce various types of lymphocytes, which protect the immune system and destroy harmful substances in the body;

Thyroid and parathyroid—are in the front of the lower neck below the larynx. The thyroid affects metabolism, body heat and bone growth, while the parathyroid affects calcium levels in the blood;

Pancreas—is centrally located behind the abdominal muscles. It secretes insulin and glucagons, which affect the absorption of glucose, the body's primary source of energy;

Adrenals—an adrenal gland is located on top of each kidney, near the middle of the back, just below the rib cage. The adrenals affect metabolism, blood pressure and saline balance;

Gonads—you know where they are and what they do.

Key: Accelerate the Frequency of Your Physiological Circuitry

This key begins with an energetic exercise in thumping the thymus, which amplifies the frequency in your glands and organs. It continues with the assimilation of violet light into your glands, organs and body systems. As you assimilate your resonance of this light into your physiological circuitry, it accelerates the electron particle spin throughout your circuit system and primes it for conscious ascension.

Allow your inner guidance to direct the pace of this key as its frequency assimilates into your physiological circuitry. You may find it necessary to accelerate and integrate one gland, organ and body system at a time. If so, ground your energy into the center of the earth-star, and when appropriate, resume with the next body system.

✡   ✡   ✡

Place your consciousness in the center of the solar heart, and energetically feel its cosmic cadence as your pulsating rhythm.... Set the intention for your light to spin at a minimum of 700,000 vibrations per mono-second throughout this key, and accelerate the frequency of your physiological circuitry.... If through birth or surgery you are missing glands or organs, intuitively sense the frequency of their etheric form....

Place your index and middle finger of one hand on the thymus.... Slowly tap your fingers to the beat of a viennese waltz—1..., 2... 3...., 1..., 2... 3...., 1..., 2... 3.... Use a firm touch as you tap the first beat, and a lighter touch with a slight delay before you tap the next 2 beats.... Repeat as necessary, until you feel this pulsating rhythm in your physical body....

Shift your awareness to your muscles, tendons and joints.... Energetically scan their physiological circuitry, and then project your light into them.... When ready, shift your awareness to the center of your bones, and thoroughly scan their marrow....

Emanate your resonance of gold-platinum light throughout the skeletal structure of your body....

Expand your awareness throughout your musculoskeletal system.... Energetically feel your light accelerate the frequency of this body system.... Take a moment and be fully present with your experience, then proceed with the acceleration of your sensory organs and their systems....

✡

Place your consciousness on your eyes, ears, nose and mouth, and assimilate violet light into these sensory organs.... Intuitively sense the frequency of the epidermis, dermis and subcutaneous layers of your skin, and synthesize your resonance of voilet light into each layer....

Expand your awareness throughout your sensory systems, and energetically feel your light accelerate the frequency of this body system.... In this moment, be fully present with your experience, then proceed with the acceleration of your nervous system....

While your consciousness is in the nervous system, intuitively sense the frequency of your pituitary, pineal and hypothalamus glands.... Assimilate violet light into each one.... Shift your awareness to your brain, and synthesize your resonance of this light into this organ....

Feel your light expand throughout your nervous system, and energetically feel it accelerate the frequency of this body system.... Take a moment and be fully present with your experience, and when ready, proceed with the acceleration of your circulatory system....

✡

Place your consciousness at your thymus and heart, and assimilate violet light into this gland and organ.... Intuitively sense the subtle flow of your bloodstream, and synthesize your own resonant pulsation of light into this lifeline....

Expand your awareness throughout your circulatory system, and energetically feel your light accelerate the frequency of this body system.... In this moment, be fully present with your experience, then proceed with the acceleration of your immune system....

While your consciousness is in the immune system, intuitively sense the frequency of your lymph nodes and spleen.... Assimilate violet light into these glands and this organ....

Feel your light expand throughout your immune system.... Energetically feel your own resonance of violet light accelerate the frequency of this body system.... Take a moment and be fully present with your experience, then proceed with the acceleration of your respiratory system....

✡

Place your consciousness at your thyroid, parathyroid and lungs, and assimilate violet light into these glands and organs.... Intuitively sense the frequency of your diaphragm, and synthesize your resonance of this light into this organ....

Expand your awareness throughout your respiratory system, and energetically feel your light accelerate the frequency of this body system.... In this moment, be fully present with your experience, then proceed with the acceleration of your digestive system....

While your consciousness is in the digestive system, intuitively sense the frequency of your pancreas, liver and gallbladder.... Assimilate violet light into this gland and these organs.... Shift your awareness to your esophagus and stomach, and synthesize your resonant pulsation of this light into these organs....

Feel your light expand throughout your digestive system.... Energetically feel your own resonance of violet light accelerate the frequency of this body system.... Take a moment and be fully present with your experience, and when ready, proceed with the acceleration of your elimination system....

✡

Place your consciousness at your adrenals, kidneys and bladder, and assimilate violet light into these glands and organ.... Shift your awareness to your intestines, and synthesize your resonance of this light into this organ....

Expand your awareness throughout your elimination system, and energetically feel your light accelerate the frequency of this body system.... In this moment, be fully present with your experience, then proceed with the acceleration of your reproductive system....

While your consciousness is in the reproductive system, intuitively sense the frequency of your gonads and reproductive organs.... Assimilate violet light into these glands and organs....

Feel your own resonance of violet light expand throughout your reproductive system.... Accelerate the frequency of this body system, and feel your light as it spins your electron particles at a minimum of 700,000 vibrations.... Take a moment and be fully present with your experience....

Energetically feel your own resonant pulsation of gold-platinum light in the center of the vesica piscis, and command its 2 overlapping discs to spin.... Amplify your electron particle spin towards 800,000 vibrations per mono-second, and feel this momentum emanate throughout your circuit system....

Shift your awareness to the center of the earth-star, and feel your light within it.... Energetically feel your light continue to accelerate, as it grounds into the main power current of your physiological circuitry....

When ready, bring your awareness to where you are in the moment, and breathe into your experience.

✿　✿　✿

Window to the Spectrum of Light

The full spectrum of light emanates an interstellar encodement, which permeates all planes of existence. There are an *infinite* number of rays of light that illuminate this spectrum, and every one radiates a specific frequency.

The full spectrum of light is partially available to human consciousness; however the range of enlightenment within the first 12 rays is fully accessible to our framework of awareness. The more we feel our own resonance of these rays flow throughout our circuit system, the more we experience transformation within us.

The first of these 12 rays comprise 2 unique groups: 7 rays of perspective and

5 rays of divine will. Each ray governs a wide range of enlightenment and emanates heightened attributes that assist us in our spiritual evolution as well as in our day-to-day life.

The more we become consciously aware of our resonant pulsations within this preliminary spectrum of light, the more sensitive we are to other subtle frequencies within the full spectrum.

Following is an overview of the first 12 rays that enlighten our awareness:

1st **Ray**—this ray of perspective radiates the principle of creation. Its light enters through the thyroid gland and emanates as auditory tones through the throat. While we assimilate this ray as our resonance of light, we enlighten our awareness and embrace our authenticity through the attributes of faith, courage, discernment, perception, spiritual strength, communication and vitality;

2nd **Ray**—emanates the principle: as above, is below. Its frequency synthesizes at the crown and emanates through the pineal gland as intuition. As we integrate the frequency of this ray, we experience enlightenment through the attributes of spiritual wisdom and illumination;

3rd **Ray**—sustains cosmic intelligence. Its light integrates through the thymus gland and emanates cosmic cadence through the solar heart. We energetically feel our light in this ray, as we enlighten our awareness, and express infinite love through the attributes of acceptance, gratitude, balance and reverence;

4th **Ray**—radiates cosmic harmony and emanates through the adrenal glands. As we synergize our resonance of light within this ray, we integrate purity through the attributes of resurrection, restoration, ascension and creation;

5th Ray—emanates an advanced perception of cosmic insight that filters through the pituitary gland. As we energetically feel our own resonance within this ray, we enlighten our awareness and experience truth through the attributes of knowledge, concentration, dedication, consecration and self-reflection;

6th Ray—sustains devotion and as it emanates through the pancreas, we experience neutrality. As we synthesize our resonant pulsation within this ray, we balance the polarization of cause and effect, and experience enlightenment through the attributes of inner peace, devotional worship, service and cosmic mission;

7th Ray—radiates oneness and emanates through the gonads. As we energetically feel our resonance of light in this ray, we enlighten our awareness and manifest freedom through the attributes of forgiveness, mercy, invocation, transmutation and infinite love;

8th Ray—this ray of divine will sustains symmetry and synthesizes balanced polarity throughout our circuit system. As we integrate the frequency of this ray, we emanate cosmic perception and experience enlightenment through the attributes of clarity, integrity and equality;

9th Ray—sustains cosmic harmony and emanates the interstellar frequency of the lightbody blueprint. While we synergize this ray of light, conscious knowing emerges and we experience enlightenment through the attributes of receptivity, certainty and synchronicity;

10th Ray—radiates infinity and emanates cosmic balance with other interplanetary civilizations. As we assimilate the frequency of this ray, we experience enlightenment and liberation through the attribute of freedom;

11th **Ray**—emanates divine purpose throughout all consciousness. While we energetically feel our resonance in this ray, we experience enlightenment and perfection through the attributes of spiritual fulfillment, enthusiasm, joy and passion;

12th **Ray**—this ray assimilates unified frequencies of light beyond this preliminary spectrum. As we synergize our light within this ray, we energetically feel enlightenment through the subtle emanation of an infinite spectrum of light that radiates beyond the scope of human understanding. To activate your remembrance of all that you are as light, begin with the key that follows the art image.

Cosmic Eye:
Window to the Spectrum of Light

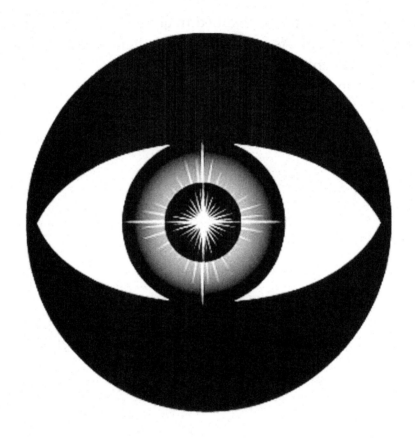

Key: Experience Enlightenment Through the 12 Rays of Light

Enlightenment through the 12 rays of light facilitates our experience of conscious ascension while in human embodiment. As you energetically feel your resonance of light within the color spectrum of these rays, allow your inner guidance to direct this pace. If it is necessary to interrupt the flow of this experience, ground your energy in the center of the earth-star and resume with the next ray, when appropriate.

✡   ✡   ✡

Place your consciousness at the cosmic eye in the center of your forehead, and envision a luminescent white light, as your resonant pulsation of light... Set the conscious intention to spin your electron particles at a minimum of 800,000 vibrations per mono-second throughout this key.... Shift your awareness to the center of the solar heart, and energetically feel its cosmic cadence as your pulsating rhythm....

Place your consciousness in the thyroid gland, located at the base of your throat, and feel your resonance of light within it.... Breathe into the color blue, and intuitively sense the frequency of this 1st ray, as it assimilates into the main power current of your spinal column.... Integrate authenticity, and emanate its attributes of faith, courage, discernment, perception, spiritual strength, communication and vitality.... When ready, shift your awareness to the 2nd ray of light....

✡

While your consciousness is in the 2nd ray, intuitively sense the frequency of the pineal gland, located in the middle of the brain, and breathe into the color yellow.... Energetically feel your own resonance of this light spin your electron particles, and emanate its pulsation throughout the main power current in your spinal column.... Integrate spiritual wisdom, and feel a greater sense of enlightenment throughout your cerebral circuitry.... In this moment breathe into your experience, and shift your awareness to the 3rd ray....

Intuitively sense the frequency of this 3rd ray, and breathe its color pink into the thymus gland, located 1 inch below the center of the clavicle.... Emanate infinite love through the attributes of acceptance, gratitude, balance and reverence.... When ready, shift your awareness to the 4th ray of light....

Place your consciousness in the 4th ray, and intuitively sense its frequency in the adrenals, located on top of each kidney near the middle of the back.... Energetically feel your own pulsation of white light, as it spins your electron particles throughout the main power current in your spinal column.... Integrate purity, and emanate its attributes of resurrection, restoration and ascension throughout your physiological circuitry.... Take a moment, and breathe into your experience, then shift your awareness to the 5th ray....

Intuitively sense the frequency of this 5th ray of light.... Breathe its color emerald green into the pituitary gland, centrally located behind the eyes in the center of the brain.... Feel the enlightenment of truth within your awareness, and emanate its attributes of knowledge, concentration, dedication, consecration and self-reflection.... When ready, shift your awareness to the 6th ray of light....

While your consciousness is in the 6th ray, intuitively sense the frequency of the pancreas, centrally located behind the abdominal muscles, and breathe into the color magenta.... Energetically feel your own pulsation of this light spin your electron particles throughout the main power current in your spinal column.... Synergize balance into all cause and effect, and assimilate its attributes of inner peace, devotional worship, service and cosmic mission into your physiological circuitry.... In this moment breathe into your experience, and shift your awareness to the 7th ray....

Place your consciousness in the 7th ray.... Breathe its color violet into the gonads, and synergize this light within your circuit system.... When ready, feel the enlightenment of freedom within your awareness, and emanate its attributes of invocation, transmutation, compassion, forgiveness and mercy.... Take a moment, and breathe into your experience, then shift your awareness to the 8th ray....

While your consciousness is in the 8th ray, assimilate the luminescent colors green-violet.... Energetically feel your own resonant frequency of this light spin your electron particles throughout your circuit system.... Synthesize heightened perception through the cosmic eye, and emanate its attributes of clarity, integrity and equality.... When ready, shift your awareness to the 9th ray of light....

Intuitively sense the frequency of this 9th ray.... Breathe into its radiant colors of blue-green, and assimilate them throughout your spinal column.... Energetically feel your own resonant pulsation of the galactic lightbody, and breathe its frequency into the main power current of your spinal column.... Synergize this frequency, and emanate the attributes of this ray's receptivity, certainty and synchronicity.... Take a moment and breathe into your experience, then shift your awareness to the 10th ray....

Place your consciousness in the 10th ray, and assimilate the color iridescent pearl into the main power current of your spinal column.... Energetically feel your own resonant pulsation of light in cosmic balance with this ray, and radiate synchronicity throughout the circuit system.... Emanate this ray's attributes of freedom and liberation throughout infinity.... In this moment, breathe into your experience, and shift your awareness to the 11th ray of light....

Intuitively sense the frequency of this 11th ray.... Breathe into its color peach, and assimilate it into the main power current of your spinal column.... Synergize perfection, and emanate its attributes of spiritual fulfillment, enthusiasm, joy and passion.... When ready, shift your awareness to the 12th ray....

While your consciousness is in the 12th ray, energetically feel your resonant pulsation of gold-platinum light in the center of the vesica piscis, and spin your electron particles at a minimum of 800,000 vibrations per mono-second.... Emanate this unified ray of light throughout the main power current in your spinal column....

Focus your awareness at the center of your forehead, and perceive this spectrum of light through the cosmic eye.... Energetically feel a greater sense of enlightenment, and expand your awareness farther into the cosmos, where it assimilates the frequencies of other infinite rays of light.... Take a moment and be consciously aware of any sensations in your physical body....

Shift your awareness to the center of the earth-star, and feel your light within it.... Energetically feel your resonant pulsation of all 12 rays of light as it grounds into your physiological circuitry....

When ready, bring your awareness to where you are in the moment, and breathe into your experience.

✿   ✿   ✿

Matrix for Solar Chakratic Circuitry

The main power current throughout the physical body sustains an intricate system of chakratic circuitry. The 12 solar gateways in this circuitry energetically interconnect with the frequencies of the 7 primary gateways in the auric field: the root, polarity, solar plexus, heart, throat, third eye and crown. These frequencies also intertwine with 21 minor gateways in the physical body. The locations of these minor gateways are: behind each eye, behind each cheekbone, the clavicle and another one an inch below it, on the inside curvature of each breast, at the gallbladder and at the spleen, and another just below it. To the right of this location, approximately 1 1/2 inches, there is another gateway, then one more at the liver, at each side of the pubic bone, in the palm of each hand, behind each knee, and at the arch of each foot. As we experience the momentum of the quantum shift, the 7 primary and 21 minor gateways refine their frequencies into their 5th dimensional blueprint.

There are many books available that contain fundamental knowledge on the primary chakratic circuitry, for those lifestreams new to the understanding of this intricate system of light. If necessary take the time to gain some knowledge before moving forward with the following exercise and key.

In this exercise there are 4 sections: transformation, transmutation, transfiguration and synergy. Each section synthesizes the primary gateways and prepares the corresponding physiological, cerebral, emotional for the assimilation of their 5th dimensional frequency. Place your consciousness on each section, in the order indicated, and energetically feel your light in these chakratic location(s). When complete declare the spoken word, *eli, eli, eli,* and synergize the attributes of their solar light within the main power current of your spinal column.

✿   ✿   ✿

Transformation—integrate the frequencies of the 7 primary gateways, and experience transformation take place in your physiological circuitry:

Root—integrates accelerated physiological circuitry,
Polarity center and throat—synthesize neutrality,
Solar plexus and third eye—integrate clarity,
Heart—assimilates free will,
Crown—integrates balance.

✡

Transmutation—synthesize the frequencies of the 7 primary gateways, and intuitively sense transmutation take place in your cerebral circuitry:

Root and throat—assimilate frequencies of accelerated circuitry,
Solar plexus and third eye—amplify inner peace and intuitive insight,
Heart—emanates love towards all,
Polarity and crown—synthesize inner balance.

Transfiguration—assimilate the frequencies of the 7 primary gateways and energetically feel these gateways transfigure throughout your emotional circuitry:

Root, polarity and solar plexus—assimilate solar chakratic frequencies,
Heart—synergizes divine will,
Throat and third eye—accelerate cosmic insight,
Crown—assimilates cosmic balance and harmony.

✡

Synergy—assimilate this unified frequency of light and emanate it throughout your circuit system:

Root, polarity and solar plexus—assimilate multidimensional frequencies,
Heart—emanates infinite love,
Throat, cosmic eye and crown—synergize unified consciousness.

Bring your own resonance of this unified frequency of light upward from the root through the main power current of your spinal column to the crown. Through conscious intention and with absolute certainty, declare the following spoken word:

"eli, eli, eli,
eli, eli, eli,
eli, eli, eli."

The frequency of this spoken word opens another energetic gateway, which is above the soul-star. This solar gateway intertwines with the cerebral circuitry in your brain, flows through the main power current of your spinal column and emanates throughout your central nervous system. Therefore, assimilation of these solar frequencies is vital for conscious ascension.

✿　✿　✿

Color Spectrum for Solar Chakratic Gateways

The rainbow spectrum of light, as we know it, consists of 7 original colors as well as infrared and ultraviolet frequencies that weave through our circuit system. As we experience the momentum of the quantum shift the frequency of this spectrum alters, and we energetically assimilate 5 additional solar gateways to the known color spectrum. Together, these additional gateways complete the 5th dimensional color spectrum for the solar chakratic gateways, each of which interconnects to the main power current in our spinal column.

Each solar gateway radiates a different frequency of light, which vibrates to specific solar emanations yet, when in absolute alignment, these 12 gateways synchronize as one.

✿　✿　✿

invisible—spiritual direction
white—restoration
opal—ascension activation
violet—transformation
ruby—cosmic light
peach—divine purpose
gold—christ-light
pink—infinite love
magenta—cosmic synergy
cobalt blue—intergalactic communication
aquamarine—cosmic insight
gold-platinum—intergalactic stargate

✿　✿　✿

The following information is an overview of the 12 solar gateways, and together with the illustration that follows, assists in the understanding of solar chakratic circuitry:

1st **Solar gateway**—is behind your knees and supports heightened spiritual direction;

2nd **Solar gateway**—located at your coccyx, it emanates white light as the seed of conscious resurrection and restoration;

3rd **Solar gateway**—is above your pubic bone, radiates opal light and supports the momentum of your conscious ascension;

4th **Solar gateway**—at your polarity center, this gateway emits violet light, supports transmutation and emanates your resonant pulsation of the spoken word, *I AM*;

5th **Solar gateway**—is below your navel, radiates ruby light and sustains divine purpose;

6th **Solar gateway**—located at your solar plexus, it emanates peach light and supports the conscious understanding of your divine purpose;

7th **Solar gateway**—is at your spleen and radiates christ-light through your own resonant pulsation of gold light;

8th **Solar gateway**—at the heart, this gateway emanates pink light and supports innate balanced love;

9th **Solar gateway**—emanates the interstellar frequency of the solar heart, which radiates infinite love and cosmic synergy through your own resonance of magenta light;

10th Solar gateway—at your clavicle, this gateway emanates cobalt blue light and synergizes intergalactic communication through the spoken word;

11th Solar gateway—is the cosmic eye, which assimilates vast insight through your own resonant frequency of aquamarine light;

12th Solar gateway—located at your crown, it radiates yellow light and emanates cosmic intelligence;

Once the frequencies of all 12 solar gateways assimilate into the main power current of your spinal column, your light naturally flows through the soul-star and enters an intergalactic stargate that vibrates to the unified frequency of gold-platinum light.

The following illustration denotes the energetic location of these solar gateways. The base of each triangle represent frequencies of interconnecting circuitry that emanate gold-platinum light.

Matrix for Solar Chakratic Circuitry

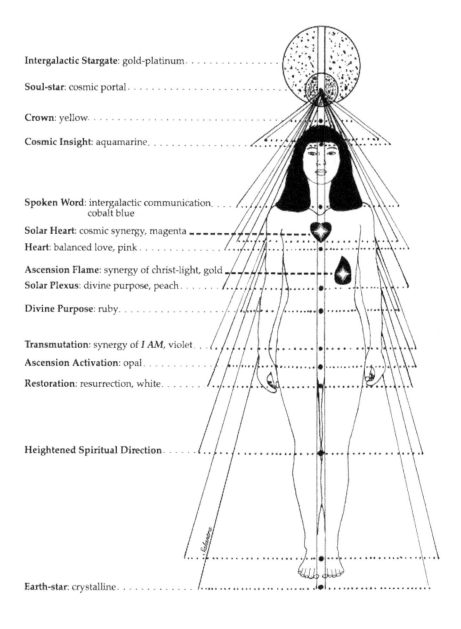

Intergalactic Stargate: gold-platinum . . . .

Soul-star: cosmic portal . . . .

Crown: yellow . . . .

Cosmic Insight: aquamarine . . . .

Spoken Word: intergalactic communication . . . .
           cobalt blue

Solar Heart: cosmic synergy, magenta ▪ ▪ ▪ ▪ ▪ ▪

Heart: balanced love, pink . . . .

Ascension Flame: synergy of christ-light, gold ▪ ▪ ▪

Solar Plexus: divine purpose, peach . . . .

Divine Purpose: ruby . . . .

Transmutation: synergy of *I AM*, violet . . . .

Ascension Activation: opal . . . .

Restoration: resurrection, white . . . .

Heightened Spiritual Direction . . . .

Earth-star: crystalline . . . .

Key: Assimilate Solar Frequencies in Your Chakratic Circuitry

In this key you intertwine solar frequencies into the primary gateways in the main power current of your spinal column. As your light flows upward through these gateways, it transfigures your primary circuitry into its counterpart, solar chakratic circuitry. If this is a new experience for you, be patient and take the time to energetically feel the sensations that flow throughout your physical body.

Allow your inner guidance to direct the assimilation of the frequencies in these solar gateways. If in any moment you find it necessary to take extra time for your experience, ground your energy into the center of the earth-star, and resume with the next gateway when appropriate. Be patient and gentle with yourself as your light assimilates the frequencies of all 12 solar gateways.

✡   ✡   ✡

Place your consciousness in the center of the solar heart, and energetically feel its cosmic cadence as your pulsating rhythm.... Shift your awareness to the main power current in your spinal column, and intuitively sense your light within it.... Set the intention for your light to spin your electron particles at a minimum of 800,000 vibrations per mono-second throughout this key....

Change your focus, and place your consciousness in the center of the earth-star, then energetically feel your light within it.... Shift your awareness to the 1st solar gateway, located behind your knees.... Intuitively sense its frequency as it supports your spiritual direction.... Energetically infuse your light into this solar gateway, and then shift your awareness to the interconnecting circuitry between the 1st and 2nd gateways.... Assimilate the frequency of this circuitry into the main power current of your spinal column, then proceed to the 2nd gateway....

✡

112

In the 2nd solar gateway, located at your coccyx, energetically feel white light in the main power current of your spinal column.... Synthesize this light and assimilate essential rejuvenation and restoration into your physical body.... Shift your awareness to the interconnecting circuitry between the 2nd and 3rd gateways, and synergize the frequency of this circuitry into your main power current.... Take a moment and be fully present with your experience, then proceed to the 3rd solar gateway located above your pubic bone.... Energetically feel your resonance of its opal light assimilate into the main power current of your spinal column....

Shift your awareness to the interconnecting circuitry between the 3rd and 4th gateways, and assimilate the frequency of its circuitry into your main power current.... When ready, proceed to the 4th solar gateway, located at your polarity center.... Energetically feel violet light in the main power current of your spinal column, and emanate your resonance of light, as *I AM*.... Shift your awareness to the interconnecting circuitry between the 4th and 5th gateways, and synergize the frequency of this circuitry.... Take a moment and be fully present with your experience, then proceed to the 5th gateway....

While your consciousness is at the 5th solar gateway, located below your navel, intuitively sense the frequency of its ruby light.... Synthesize this light into the main power current of your spinal column, and emanate your spiritual purpose.... Place your consciousness at the interconnecting circuitry between the 5th and 6th gateways, and energetically feel this frequency in the central meridian of your spinal column.... When ready, proceed to the 6th solar gateway, located at your solar plexus.... Energetically feel peach light in the main power current of your spinal column, and be aware of the conscious understanding of your divine purpose.... Shift your awareness to the interconnecting circuitry between the 6th and 7th gateways, and synergize the frequency of this circuitry into your main power current.... Take a moment and be fully present with your experience, then proceed to the 7th gateway....

While your consciousness is at the 7th solar gateway, located at your spleen, feel your own resonant pulsation of christ-light in the center of the ascension flame.... Synergize your light in the main power current of your spinal column.... When ready, shift your awareness to the interconnecting circuitry between the 7th and 8th gateways, and energetically feel this frequency in the central meridian of your spinal column, then proceed to the 8th gateway....

In the 8th solar gateway, or physical heart, energetically feel pink light in the main power current of your spinal column, and synthesize balanced love into this energetic center.... When ready, shift your awareness to the interconnecting circuitry between the 8th and 9th gateways, and synergize the frequency of this circuitry.... Take a moment and be fully present with your experience, then proceed to the 9th solar gateway, located at the solar heart.... Energetically feel your own resonance of magenta light emanate infinite love into the main power current of your spinal column....

Place your consciousness at the interconnecting circuitry between the 9th and 10th gateways, and energetically feel your own resonance of this frequency in the central meridian of your spinal column.... Proceed to the 10th solar gateway, located at your clavicle, and energetically feel cobalt blue light assimilate intergalactic communication through your throat.... When ready, shift your awareness to the interconnecting circuitry between the 10th and 11th gateways, and synergize the frequency of this circuitry.... Take a moment and be fully present with your experience, then proceed to the 11th gateway....

✡

While your consciousness is at the 11th solar gateway, located at the cosmic eye, intuitively sense your own resonance of aquamarine light, and experience an expanded perception of cosmic insight.... Shift your awareness to the interconnecting circuitry between the 11th and 12th gateways, and feel this frequency in the central meridian of your spinal column.... When ready, place your consciousness in the 12th solar gateway, located above the crown, and energetically feel a unified resonant pulsation of yellow light intertwine with the frequency in the main power current....

Project your light through the soul-star to the other side of its intergalactic stargate, and at the same time shift your awareness to the sacrum.... Spin your electron particles at a minimum of 800,000 vibrations.... Energetically feel your resonant pulsation of gold-platinum light in the center of the vesica piscis, and command its 2 overlapping discs to spin.... Amplify your electron particle spin towards 900,000 vibrations per mono-second, and feel your frequency accelerate within your chakratic circuitry.... Synergize the frequencies of all 12 solar gateways throughout the main power current of your spinal column....

Shift your awareness to the center of the earth-star, and feel your light within it.... Energetically feel your light in all 12 solar gateways as it grounds into your physiological circuitry....

When ready, bring your awareness to where you are in the moment, and breathe into your experience.

✡   ✡   ✡

Interstellar Elixir of the Solar Heart

The interstellar elixir of the solar heart emits a pulsating cosmic cadence that radiates throughout star systems within star systems, galaxies within galaxies, and universes within universes. It nourishes the essence of all life and transmits a unified frequency of light that supports the spiritual nexus of universal brotherhood: as above, is below.

While we energetically feel its cosmic cadence as our pulsating rhythm, our human heart beats to this natural rhythm of cosmic synchronicity.

Key: Experience Your Own Pulsating Rhythm

In this key your light assimilates the interstellar elixir of infinite love as it emanates from the solar heart and pulsates to cosmic synchronicity. As you energetically feel your own pulsating rhythm within your physiological circuitry you sense your resonance of light as it radiates from the galactic core.

✦   ✦   ✦

With great reverence, place your consciousness in the center of the solar heart, and energetically feel its cosmic cadence as your resonant pulsation.... In this moment, be fully present with your experience....

Shift your awareness to the sacrum, and spin your electron particles at a minimum of 900,000 vibrations per mono-second, and feel this frequency throughout your circuit system.... With absolute certainty, declare the following spoken word:

Throughout the sphere of oneness,
is the radiance and illumination,
of our own resonance of light.

Within the solar heart,
is an interstellar elixir,
that synchronizes our pulsation of light.

As the essence of infinite love,
our rhythm pulsates to our inner core, and
we dance of the essence of this cosmic cadence.

We are all-that-is.

Energetically feel your resonant pulsation of gold-platinum light in the center of the vesica piscis, and command its 2 overlapping discs to spin.... Amplify your electron particle spin towards 1,000,000 vibrations per mono-second, and feel this frequency accelerate the main power current of your spinal column....

When you are complete with your experience, shift your awareness to your human heart.... Take a moment and be fully present with the energetic sensation that emanates throughout your physical body....

Shift your awareness to the center of the earth-star, and feel your light within it.... Energetically feel your own pulsation of cosmic cadence, and ground it into your physiological circuitry....

When ready, bring your awareness to where you are in the moment, and be fully present with your experience.

✿   ✿   ✿

Interstellar Matrix for the Solar Heart

Within me is full consious awaremess
of my own resonant pulsation
as christ-light

Threshold of the Ascension Flame

The light of another dawn is on our doorstep and supports us as we assimilate its increased magnitude into our consciousness. Wherever we are in the progress of our spiritual evolution, continual energetic acceleration of our circuit system is at the heart of ascension.

The ascension flame activates rebirth and we energetically feel it in the spleen, which is the anatomical location for this flame. This organ is the holding vessel for the frequency of christ-light, *meshiah m'shi shi* [m-she' ah m-she' she'], which supports our physical body throughout the ascension experience. As we experience this fusion, we awaken cosmic codes that are in our blood; the frequency within these codes interconnect with an interstellar grid that permeates the etheric grid of earth, activates dna stellar substance, and opens sealed records of truth that reside deep within us. Our own resonance of christ-light serves as mediator for the assimilation of abstract cosmic intelligence and emanates advanced knowledge to the conscious mind.

As we experience our momentum of the quantum shift, we amplify our pulsation of light within the ascension flame, which further accelerates the resonant frequency within the spleen. Continual acceleration of the electron particle spin amplifies every atom, molecule and cell of our physiological circuitry. As we increase our vibrations per mono-second beyond 1,000,000, the ascension flame further expands to the appropriate magnitude that supports this increase in frequency.

Although the ascension flame fluctuates in its magnitude, it is inextinguishable and sustains the brilliant luminescence of 3 intertwining plumes of light. Each plume vibrates to a specific frequency and color: blue, magenta or gold. On one side of the center plume is the blue plume, which naturally synergizes divine right action. On the other side of the center plume is the magenta plume, which emanates infinite love. The center plume is gold in color, and as its unified frequency energetically increases in our spleen we synergize our own resonance of christ-light.

Our ascension experience enables us to cross several thresholds in consciousness and refine the way in which we live life. Are you ready to energetically feel your own resonance of christ-light?

Key: Experience Christ-Light, as Your Light

The energetic resonance of christ-light enters your physiological circuitry through the soul-star or 8th solar gateway, and assimilates into your physiological circuitry through the frequency of the ascension flame in the spleen. In the following key you feel this synergy through 3 energetic plumes of radiance that reside within the ascension flame.

✿   ✿   ✿

Envision a sacred chamber of light that illuminates a radiant throne in its center…. When ready, assume your rightful position on this throne, and feel your own resonant pulsation of gold light emanate throughout your physical body….

Through the cosmic eye, see a spiritual crown inlaid with 12 jewels of light, and place it on your head…. Above this crown envision a chalice filled with gold light…. Tip the chalice, and energetically feel your own resonance of christ-light flow through the soul-star, into the main power current of your spinal column, and down to your spleen….

With your consciousness in the center of your spleen, envision the ascension flame on an altar with 3 plumes of radiant light that are blue, magenta and gold in color…. Place your consciousness inside this flame, and feel your own resonant pulsation of light in the blue plume…. Shift your awareness to the magenta plume, and energetically feel the light that radiates from it…. When ready, shift your awareness to the center of the gold plume, and energetically feel your own resonant pulsation of christ-light emanate from its core....

Sustain your energy within the gold plume, and shift your focus to the soul-star or 8th solar gateway above your head.... Through your intention, declare the following spoken word, and repeat the last line 12 times:

> *"I AM* christ-light, and
> awaken stellar codes within my blood that
> emanate a resonant pulsation of light throughout my body.
> *"*m'shia m'shi shi" [m-she' ah m-she' she']

As this solar gateway fully opens, energetically feel your resonance of christ-light in your spleen.... Declare the following spoken word at least 3 times, and be certain to breathe in and out after each time:

> "zohar christou" [zo-har chris-too]

Synergize the encodement of light within these spoken words, and assimilate their frequencies into the main power current of your spinal column.... Feel your light spin your electron particles into a vortex of energy that flows throughout this main power current.... Breathe this vortex into your spleen and spin it at a minimum of 1,000,000 vibrations per mono-second.... Take a moment and be fully present with your experience....

Energetically feel your own resonant pulsation of gold-platinum light in the center of the vesica piscis, and command its 2 overlapping discs to spin.... Amplify your electron particle spin towards 1,100,000 vibrations per mono-second, and feel this acceleration in your spleen....

Shift your awareness to the center of the earth-star, and feel your light within it.... Energetically feel your own resonance of christ-light, and ground it into your physiological circuitry....

When ready, bring your awareness to where you are in the moment, and breathe into your experience.

✡   ✡   ✡

Matrix for the Ascension Flame

New Blueprint and Its Configuration of Light

As biological evolution progresses exponentially, and we consciously experience complete rejuvenation and restoration from our imperfect creations, we progress towards the full assimilation of a new blueprint. The inevitability of this synergy supports the future development of our interplanetary civilization on the new earth; therefore, it is beneficial that we have a basic understanding of the advanced energetic technology that facilitates this infusion.

The atom is a stable configuration of energy that emanates a unique electron frequency, known as an atomic cloud. A single atom comprises 4 different energies: the neutron, the duatron, the photon, and the electron. The electron, the 4th energy is the unification of the other 3 and represents fusion. The neutron is conscious heart energy, the duatron is electrical energy through the palms of the hands, the proton is magnetic energy and the electron is adhesive energy. This information is based on spiritual knowing as well as healing experiences with vibrational frequencies, rather than on the capability of science to measure.

Electrons are subatomic particles that live inside atoms, and they obey quantum physical laws. They are electronically charged at the center of the atoms that they occupy. Electrons have a negative charge (-) and nuclei have a positive charge (+); therefore, the electrons are held together by the electrical force of the attraction between them and generate an infinite amount of energy.

The new blueprint sustains a configuration of light that emanates geometric encodements into atoms and molecules. Each molecule is an undulating frequency in the center of each atom, yet the master molecule that contains the original genetic blueprint of divinity is dna. Macromolecules of dna are pairs of molecules that intertwine and form a double helix. Therefore, dna is the genetic structure of the master molecule of life, and its blueprint of divinity is in the atoms, molecules and nuclei of our cells. This new blueprint transfigures dna from a carbon-based density to a transparent, geometric, light-based frequency comprised of icosahedron (water), and dodecahedron (ether).

As we experience the momentum of the quantum shift our 2-strand dna unbundles and activates the original configurations of dna strands. This activation naturally regenerates their 10-strands out of a dormant state and restores all of our genetic encodement. Our physical body synergizes its new blueprint by energetically transmitting the frequencies of these geometric encodements into our physiological circuitry, as well as our cellular circuitry. The energetic transfer for this blueprint is assimilated into the body through the pituitary, or master gland and emanates through our eyes, our hands or our voice.

Configuration of 5th Dimensional Physiological Circuitry

We each have unique requirements in order to maintain health and vitality in our lives; and in the new matrix of life, the length of our lifespan is a conscious preference.

Although we are responsible for the way in which we assimilate the interstellar substance ether into our physiological circuitry we are unable to fully perceive the significance of its highly developed function, or how it facilitates in the pro-creation of the new 5th dimensional species.

Assimilation of this etheric form of ether, into the main power current of our spinal column, synergizes multiple frequencies of advanced energetic technology throughout the human circuit system. This technology sustains the essential encodement that transfigures our circuitry and prevents premature dematerialization to other dimensions beyond the 5th.

As our physiological circuitry synergizes the configuration of this new blueprint it is influenced by a complex interface between solar and lunar cycles. Therefore, as we assimilate the interstellar substance ether into our endocrine glands: the pituitary, hypothalamus, pineal, thyroid, parathyroid, thymus, adrenals, pancreas and reproductive glands, as well as our organs and body systems, our physical body appears more youthful regardless of our biological age.

The following information is an overview of 5th dimensional physiological circuitry. If necessary, review the prior section, *Matrix for Accelerated Physiological Circuitry* for the precise anatomical location of the glands, organs and their body system, before you use the key, *Assimilate the New Blueprint*, as it energetically synergizes an enhanced encodement into the physiological circuitry.

> **Musculoskeletal system**—this new blueprint ultimately facilitates transfiguration of the human form into a new skeletal structure that is 8 to 10 feet tall. The rib cage in this new system is a flexible cartilage that expands as the diaphragm expands, which enables our muscles to naturally move with this new structure;

> **Sensory systems**—in the new matrix of life the range for all sensory systems is greatly expanded. The receptors in our skin glow with a golden radiance and emanate our ecstatic love for life. Our visual sight enhances through the depth of intergalactic insight and as a result, our eyes reveal our own resonance of light, which sparkles with varying shades of color. Our ability to hear is acute and we tune into subtle frequencies of sound, tones and overtones. Our sense of smell is extremely sharp therefore, we prefer aromatic senses. The new sensation of taste increases as we instantly recognize the distinct flavor of food. Through the sense of enhanced touch, we transfer and receive vibrational frequencies of light.

> **Primary endocrine glands and nervous system**—this new blueprint sustains 3 cerebral glands in the brain, which enables us to assimilate the interstellar substance ether into the pituitary and pineal glands. This substance energetically accelerates the frequency of the pineal and hypothalamus, which enables us to experience the ultimate state of regeneration;

Thymus and circulatory system—synchronize the cosmic cadence of the solar heart as the pulsating rhythm of our human heart. The new blueprint for the heart sustains additional etheric glands that modulate its heart rate and emanate an advanced form of light into the bloodstream;

Lymph nodes and immune system—unlike the human immune system, the new blueprint for the immune system transfigures our lymphatic system and enhances the production of new lymphocytes;

Thyroid, parathyroid and respiratory system—the new blueprint for the thyroid and parathyroid glands emanates our voice as the voice of divinity. The geometric encodement for the lungs, in conjunction with the diaphragm, energetically assimilates the interstellar substance ether and water, and provides oxygen, which the respiratory and circulatory systems extend throughout our circuitry;

Pancreas and digestive system—the new blueprint for the pancreas sustains additional etheric glands that convert fat to natural sugar so that we have more energy. The blueprint for the liver and gallbladder transfigures ancient residue into the frequency of infinite love. Assimilation of new glands into the digestive system secrete natural enzymes into this body system;

Adrenals and elimination system—the blueprint for the adrenals transfigures the metabolic rate in our body. The new encodement for our kidneys and bladder supports the transmutation of fluids, and modulates water retention—this indicates that a quantum shift in frequency occurs in the body. Therefore, the new blueprint for our intestines transfigures the way in which we eliminate intake;

Gonads and reproductive system—this new blueprint is unlike its human counterpart. Its gonads and reproductive organs have an additional etheric gland under the coccyx, which grounds the 5th dimensional blueprint to where we are on earth.

This gland enhances divine union during intimacy, as we experience the ultimate expression of tantra. For those lifestreams who choose procreation, their intimate sexual union culminates in the birth of a fully conscious lifestream.

Key: Assimilate the New Blueprint

As your physiological circuitry embodies its new blueprint, you assimilate the encodement of an advanced configuration of light. In this key your crystalline hands implant the interstellar substance ether into the glands and organs of your physiological circuitry. Then, you energetically overlay the new configuration into each body system with the assistance of your crystalline fingertips, and seal its grid with your own resonance of gold-platinum light. Once the overlay of each configuration is fully assimilated and the synergy of all the body systems is complete throughout your physiological circuitry, you experience profound rejuvenation and restoration throughout your physical body.

Due to the encodement of light in this key, assimilation of its new blueprint depends on your innate ability to synergize its frequency. It is suggested that you read this key several times to familiarize yourself with its substance, and only when you feel you are ready, overlay the new configuration of one body system at a time, or as your inner guidance directs you.

Be mindful of energetic overload or the feeling of overwhelm in your awareness. If in any moment you require extra time to synergize your experience, ground your energy in the center of the earth-star, and resume when ready. Be fully present with the sensations that arise in your physical body, and remember, complete synergy occurs in its own time.

Throughout this key your light continues to naturally spin your electron particles at a minimum of 1,100,000 vibrations per mono-second throughout this key.

✿　✿　✿

Energetically feel the cosmic cadence of the solar heart, as your pulsating rhythm.... With great reverence for your innate ability to assimilate the new blueprint, enter the depth of your own awareness.... While in your sacred space, envision your hands transfigure their physical structure into their crystalline substance, and emanate your own resonant pulsation of gold-platinum light from your fingertips.... With absolute certainty, set the intention for your crystalline hands to first assist you with the implant of the interstellar substance ether and further assist you with the overlay of the new configuration of light into your physiological circuitry....

Shift your awareness to your muscles, tendons and joints.... Energetically scan their physiological circuitry, then project your light into them.... When ready, shift your awareness to the center of your bones, and thoroughly scan their marrow.... Emanate your resonance of gold-platinum light throughout the skeletal structure of your body....

Expand your awareness throughout your musculoskeletal system.... Through your intention envision your crystalline hands implant the substance ether into your muscles, tendons, joints, bone marrow as well as this entire body system.... Intuitively sense the frequency for the new configuration of your musculoskeletal system.... With your crystalline hands, energetically overlay the new configuration for this system into your physiological circuitry, and through your fingertips, seal its grid with your resonance of gold-platinum light.... Take a moment and be fully present with the frequency of this configuration as it energetically assimilates into this system.... When ready, proceed to your sensory organs and their systems....

131

While your consciousness is at each of the sensory organs, intuitively sense the frequency of your eyes, ears, nose, mouth and skin.... Scan their physiological circuitry, and when ready, project your light into them.... Shift your awareness to the epidermis, dermis and subcutaneous layers of your skin, and energetically scan their circuitry.... Synthesize your light into these areas of your body, and energetically feel expansion in the range of your sensory systems....

Project your awareness throughout your sensory systems of sight, hearing, smell, taste and touch, and feel your light emanate through your eyes, ears, nose, mouth and skin.... Through conscious intention, envision your crystalline hands implant the interstellar substance ether into these glands, organs and their systems.... Continue to overlay the new configuration for your sensory system into your physiological circuitry, and through your fingertips, seal this grid with your own resonant pulsation of gold-platinum light.... In this moment, be fully present with your experience of this assimilation, then proceed to your nervous system....

Place your consciousness in your pituitary, pineal and hypothalamus.... Scan their circuitry, and when ready, project your resonance of light into these glands.... Shift your awareness to your brain, and scan the circuitry of this organ.... Continue to scan downward to the base of the skull, and into the medulla.... Energetically feel the interstellar substance ether, activate additional etheric glands into your cerebal circuitry....

Expand your awareness throughout your nervous system.... Through your intention, envision your crystalline hands implant the interstellar substance ether into your pituitary, pineal, hypothalamus, brain and entire nervous system.... Continue to overlay this new configuration into your physiological circuitry, and through your fingertips, seal its grid with your resonance of gold-platinum light.... Take a moment, and be fully present with the frequency of this configuration as it energetically assimilates into this system.... When ready, proceed to your circulatory system.....

While your consciousness is at the circulatory system, energetically feel the frequency of your thymus and human heart.... Scan their physiological circuitry, and when ready, project your light into them.... Energetically feel your heart rate modulate to its new rhythm, and emanate this cosmic pulsation throughout your physiological circuitry.... Shift your awareness to your bloodstream, and energetically scan its circuitry.... Synthesize your light throughout this lifeline, and feel the sensation of regeneration flowing through your veins....

Project your awareness throughout your circulatory system, and feel your light within it.... With your crystalline hands implant the substance ether into your thymus, human heart and entire circulatory system.... Continue to overlay the new configuration for your circulatory system into your physiological circuitry, and through your fingertips, seal this grid with gold-platinum light.... In this moment be fully present with your experience of this assimilation, and then proceed to your immune system....

Place your consciousness in your lymph nodes.... Scan their circuitry, and when ready, project your light into them.... Shift your awareness to your spleen, and scan the circuitry of this organ.... While your consciousness is in the spleen, emanate your resonant pulsation of christ-light throughout your physiological circuitry....

Expand your awareness throughout your immune system.... With your crystalline hands implant the interstellar substance ether into your lymph nodes, spleen, and immune system.... Continue to overlay this new configuration into your physiological circuitry, and through your fingertips, seal its grid with your own resonance of gold-platinum light.... Take a moment and be fully present with the frequency of this configuration as it energetically assimilates into this system.... When ready, proceed to your respiratory system....

While your consciousness is at the respiratory system, energetically feel the frequency of your thyroid, parathyroid and lungs.... Scan their physiological circuitry, and when ready, project your light into them.... Energetically feel your own pulsation of this 5th dimensional frequency emanate the voice of divinity as your voice.... Shift your awareness to your diaphragm, and energetically scan its circuitry.... Synthesize your light into this organ, and feel it assimilate into your physiological circuitry....

Project your awareness throughout your respiratory system, and feel your light within it.... With your crystalline hands implant the substance ether into your thyroid, parathyroid, lungs and entire respiratory system.... Continue to overlay the new configuration for your respiratory system into your physiological circuitry, and through your fingertips, seal this grid with your resonant pulsation of gold-platinum light.... In this moment, be fully present with your experience of this assimilation, and then proceed to your digestive system....

Place your consciousness in your pancreas, liver, gallbladder and stomach.... Scan their circuitry, and when ready, project your light into them.... Expand your awareness throughout your digestive system.... With your crystalline hands implant the interstellar substance ether into the pancreas, liver, gallbladder, stomach and entire digestive system....

Intuitively sense the frequency of the new configuration for your digestive system.... With your crystalline hands, energetically overlay the new configuration into your physiological circuitry, and through your fingertips, seal its grid with gold-platinum light.... Take a moment and be fully present with the frequency of this configuration as it energetically assimilates into this system.... When ready, proceed to your elimination system....

While your consciousness is at the elimination system, energetically feel the frequency of your adrenals, kidneys and bladder.... Scan their physiological circuitry, and when ready, project your light into them.... Energetically feel this frequency emanate a heightened metabolic rate in your adrenals, refine the secretion from the kidneys into the bloodstream, and transmute fluids from your physiological circuitry.... Shift your awareness to your intestines, and energetically scan its circuitry.... Synthesize your light into this organ, and energetically feel the substance ether transfigure all nutrients to nourish your body in a new way....

Project your awareness throughout your elimination system, and feel your light within it.... With your crystalline hands implant the substance ether into your adrenals, kidneys, bladder and entire elimination system.... Continue to overlay this new configuration into your physiological circuitry, and through your fingertips, seal this grid with your own resonance of gold-platinum light.... In this moment, be fully present with your experience of this assimilation, and then proceed to your reproductive system....

Place your consciousness in your gonads and reproductive organs.... Scan their circuitry, and when ready, project your light into them.... Energetically feel the substance ether implant a new gland under your coccyx....

Expand your awareness throughout your reproductive system.... With your crystalline hands implant the interstellar substance ether into your gonads, reproductive organs and their system.... Continue to overlay the new configuration for your reproductive system into your physiological circuitry, and through your fingertips, seal its grid with your resonant pulsation gold-platinum light.... Take a moment and be fully present with the frequency of this configuration as it energetically assimilates into this system....

Feel your light spin your electron particles at a minimum of 1,100,000 vibrations and experience rejuvenation and restoration throughout all your body systems.... Energetically feel your own resonance of gold-platinum light in the center of the vesica piscis, and command its 2 overlapping discs to spin.... Amplify your electron particle spin towards 1,200,000 vibrations per mono-second, and feel your light accelerate within your circuit system.... In this moment, be fully present with your experience....

Shift your awareness to the center of the earth-star, and feel your light within it.... Energetically feel the encodement of this new blueprint fully embody into your physiological circuitry....

When ready, bring your awareness to where you are in the moment, and breathe into your experience.

✿   ✿   ✿

Configuration for Cellular Circuitry

Cells are consecrated by a centrifugal force that sustains frequencies of ultraviolet and infrared light. Each cell is a micro-universe within you and acts as a neurotransmitter that translates innate wisdom through energetic currents. It is these currents that prime this circuitry for its new configuration.

The energetic adhesion required for this new configuration creates a 0 point in the nuclei of the cells, where the cell shape shifts from the chromosome state, which is material, to a centramer, which is non-material. As our cells embody their new air-based prototype, they unlock consciousness in their nuclei and naturally regenerate their components.

These highly advanced components comprise complex fundamentals, which are essential for the transfiguration of nuclei. Through our chromosomes, we transform dna that contains the linear body of the cells nuclei; through our cells, we transmute the nuclei into electric energy; through the molecules, highly advanced energetic technology transfigures the nuclei in atoms. Transfiguration within atomic nuclei enhances the procreation of a new species.

Do you accept that your cells already sustain the ability to synergize their new configuration? Are you ready to experience full remembrance within every cell of our body?

Key: Fusion of 5th Dimensional Cells

In this key your cells energetically assimilate a new configuration of light into their nuclei. With your crystalline hands you implant the interstellar substance ether into your cells, and overlay the new configuration of light as indicated. Once this configuration is fully assimilated and full synergy is complete within your cellular circuitry, you experience restoration within your physical body.

Due to the encodement of light in this key, assimilation depends on your innate ability to synergize its frequency. It is suggested that you read this key several times to familiarize yourself with its substance, and only when you feel you are ready, overlay their new configuration of light. This prevents an energetic overload throughout your circuit system as well as excessive overwhelm in your awareness. Repeat this key when appropriate.

If in any moment you require extra time to assimilate the frequency of this configuration, ground your energy in the center of the earth-star, and resume when ready. Be fully present with the sensations that arise in your physical body and remember complete synergy occurs in its own time.

Throughout this key, your resonant pulsation of light naturally spins your electron particles at a minimum of 1,200,000 vibrations per mono-second.

✧ ✧ ✧

Energetically feel the cosmic cadence of the solar heart, as your pulsating rhythm.... With absolute certainty, set the intention to implant the substance ether, and overlay the new configuration into your cellular circuitry....

Shift your awareness to one of your cells, scan the circuitry of its nucleus, and energetically clear this cell with your light.... Use your crystalline hands to implant the substance ether into this cell.... Energetically overlay the new configuration, and allow your original 12-strand dna to transform the nucleus of this cell.... Through your fingertips, seal this cell with your resonant pulsation of gold-platinum light....

Place your consciousness within the master cell in your pituitary gland.... Scan this cell with your crystalline hands, and implant the interstellar substance ether into its nucleus.... Energetically overlay the new configuration, and synthesize electric energy in the nucleus of this cell.... Through your fingertips, seal this cell with your resonance of gold-platinum light....

Expand your consciousness throughout the nuclei of *all* your cells.... Envision these cells as a micro-universe within your circuitry.... With your crystalline hands, implant the substance ether, and then energetically overlay the new configuration of light into these cells.... Through your fingertips seal your cellular circuitry with your resonance of gold-platinum light....

Energetically feel the air-based configuration throughout your cellular circuitry.... Through conscious intention and with absolute certainty, declare the following spoken word:

> "The nuclei of my cells
> synergize an air-based configuration of light, and
> emanate their new encodement.
> So be it. It is done."

Feel your light spin your electron particles at a minimum of 1,200,000 vibrations.... Energetically feel your resonant pulsation of gold-platinum light in the center of the vesica piscis, and command its 2 overlapping discs to spin....

Amplify your electron particle spin towards 1,300,000 vibrations per mono-second, and feel your own frequency of light accelerate within your circuit system....

Shift your awareness to the center of the earth-star, and feel your light within it.... Intuitively sense the frequency of your new encodement, and ground it into your physiological circuitry....

When ready, bring your awareness to where you are in the moment, and breathe into your experience.

✡   ✡   ✡

Templates of Subtle Circuitry

As with all things that exist beyond our scope of understanding, there are an infinite number of templates within other templates.

Subtle circuitry comprises etheric templates that emanate resonant pulsations of light throughout the unified circuit system; therefore, this intricate system of circuitry modulates our light as it flows from the life-sustaining silver cord, through the soul-star, into the main power current and throughout our physiological circuitry.

In this system of circuitry there are a minimum of 15 templates recognized by conscious masters on earth. Our ability to intuitively sense our own resonance of light within these 15 templates is truly dependent upon the amplification of our electron particle spin. While our own resonance of light continuously flows in and out of these templates, we are usually unconscious of this momentum.

Each template acts as a transducer and sustains frequencies, as well as luminescent and translucent light with hues that are interspersed with sparks of multicolored light. As you energetically feel your own resonant pulsation within these frequencies, the amplification of your light ranges from 1,300,000 to 2,300,000 vibrations per mono-second.

The following is a general overview on 15 of the templates in the system of subtle circuitry:

Etheric—maintains the foundational structure for all the templates throughout this subtle circuit system;

Astral—comprises the outdated imprint of complex archetypal forces that manifest as part of 3rd dimensional reality. This template is the transforming crucible through which all energy passes and ascends through the heart as spiritual awareness;

Egoic—synthesizes intellectual thoughts that emanate from cerebral mind activity;

Causal—emanates streams of light around your body, which appear like a network of threads. It facilitates conscious awareness of higher self, and supports the resonant pulsations of light that flow through the main power current in your spinal column;

Electromagnetic—supports the grid of light that maintains the human circuit system. Synergy of this template unifies your resonant pulsations of light in the etheric, astral, egoic and causal templates;

Atmic—emanates the frequency of christ-light, meshiah m'shi shi, as your light, and modulates it throughout your circuitry;

Logoic—assimilates conscious knowing into your awareness, and personifies unified consciousness;

Monadic—protects the sacred knowledge of your soul's evolution and stores it in the hall of akashic records. It also aligns dna into its original configuration of energy;

Epi-kinetic—sustains a centrifugal geometric force of cosmic pulsations that transfigure atoms, molecules and cells into their new blueprint;

Eka—modulates the language of light and assimilates geometric codes into your awareness. The frequency of this template facilitates your alchemy of conscious mastery;

Oversoul—emanates a resonant pulsation of light that facilitates inner communion while in human embodiment;

Christed-oversoul—sustains your resonant frequency of christ-light and assimilates this encodement throughout your circuit system;

Adam kadmon—is the epitome of perfection, as *adam kadmon elohim* [adam kad-mon e-lo-heem'], in physical form. This template of kabbalistic consciousness emanates its light through the sefirahs on the tree of life. Synergy of your light within this template completes the ascension experience while in human embodiment;

Zohar—synergizes the androgynous consciousness of yhvh. Awareness of your resonant pulsation in this template depends on the attainment of many thresholds in consciousness, as it facilitates remembrance of other interplanetary civilizations while in human embodiment;

Gematrian—synergizes the androgynous consciousness of shekinah.

This template sustains mathematical codes of sacred geometry that facilitate complete transfiguration of your circuit system into its new blueprint.

Key: Synergize Resonant Pulsations of Subtle Circuitry

In this key you synergize your own resonance of light within subtle circuitry. As in the previous 2 keys, with the assistance of your crystalline hands, you overlay the interstellar substance ether, implant the new configuration for each template and seal it with your own resonance of gold-platinum light. Once each overlay is fully assimilated and synergy throughout your physiological circuitry is complete, you energetically feel the fusion of all the circuit systems, as a unified system of light.

Due to the advanced encodement in this key, synergy of this subtle system depends on your innate ability to energetically feel your resonant pulsation of light within each template. Review this key several times to familiarize yourself with its substance, and only when you feel ready, overlay each configuration as your inner guidance directs you.

Be mindful of energetic overload or the feeling of overwhelm. If in any moment you require extra time to synergize your experience, ground your energy in the center of the earth-star, and resume when ready. Be fully present with the sensations that arise in your physical body, and remember, complete synergy occurs in its own time.

Throughout this key your light naturally accelerates your electron particle spin in increments, beginning at 1,300,000 and amplifying to 2,000,000 vibrations per mono-second at the end of this key.

✿   ✿   ✿

With great reverence, energetically feel the cosmic cadence of the solar heart, as your pulsating rhythm....

Shift your awareness to encompass all the templates in this circuit system, and simultaneously remain present with your own resonant pulsation of light.... Begin with the etheric, astral, egoic and causal templates....

Place your consciousness at the etheric template, and intuitively sense the frequency of its foundational structure.... Project your light into it, energetically scan its circuitry, and feel your resonant pulsation of light within this template.... Shift your awareness to the astral template, and scan its circuitry.... Feel your light release the remembrance of archetypical forces.... Move your awareness to the egoic template, scan its circuitry, and synthesize its thoughtforms.... Shift your awareness to the causal template, scan it, and energetically feel your resonant pulsation of light within it....

Expand your light to encompass these 4 templates.... With your crystalline hands, emanate gold-platinum light from your fingertips, and implant the interstellar substance ether into the main power current of your spinal column.... Energetically overlay the new configuration for these templates into the main power current of your spinal column, and through your fingertips, seal each template with your resonant pulsation of gold-platinum light....

Feel your light spin your electron particles at a minimum of 1,300,000 vibrations per mono-second.... Energetically feel your resonant pulsation of gold-platinum light in the center of the vesica piscis, and command its 2 overlapping discs to spin.... Amplify your electron particle spin towards 1,400,000 vibrations, and feel your light amplify the frequency of your circuit system....

Take a moment and synergize the frequencies of all 4 templates throughout the main power current of your spinal column.... Be fully present with your experience, and when ready, proceed to the electromagnetic template....

✡

Place your consciousness at the electromagnetic template, and energetically feel your resonant pulsation of light within it.... Scan the circuitry of this template, and with your crystalline hands implant the interstellar substance ether into the main power current of your spinal column.... Energetically overlay the new configuration for this template into your physiological circuitry, and through your fingertips, seal it with your light....

Feel your light spin your electron particles at a minimum of 1,400,000 vibrations per mono-second.... Energetically feel your resonance of gold-platinum light in the center of the vesica piscis, and command its 2 overlapping discs to spin.... Amplify your particle spin towards 1,500,000 vibrations, and feel your light accelerate throughout your circuit system....

In this moment, emanate your own resonant pulsation of this template throughout the central meridian of your spinal column, and then shift your awareness to the atmic template....

While your consciousness is at the atmic template, scan its circuitry, and energetically feel your resonance of christ-light within it.... Shift your awareness to the logoic template, project your light into it, and scan its circuitry.... When ready, place your consciousness at the monadic template, project your light into it, and scan its circuitry.... With your crystalline hands implant the substance ether into the main power current of your spinal column....

Expand your light to encompass the configuration of all 3 templates: atmic, logoic and monadic.... With your crystalline hands, energetically overlay these new configurations into your physiological circuitry, and through your fingertips, seal each one with gold-platinum light....

Feel your light spin your electron particles at a minimum of 1,500,000 vibrations.... Energetically feel your resonant pulsation of gold-platinum light in the center of the vesica piscis, and command its 2 overlapping discs to spin.... Amplify your electron particle spin towards 1,600,000 vibrations per mono-second, and feel your light accelerate throughout your circuit system....

Take a moment and synergize the frequencies of these 3 templates throughout the main power current of your spinal column.... Be fully present with your experience, and when ready, shift your awareness to the epi-kinetic template....

Place your consciousness at the epi-kinetic template, scan its circuitry, and energetically feel your resonance of light within it.... Shift your awareness to the eka template, scan its circuitry, and assimilate its geometric codes.... With your crystalline hands implant the interstellar substance ether into the main power current of your spinal column.... Energetically overlay the new configuration for these 2 templates, and through your fingertips, seal each one with your light....

Feel your light spin your electron particles at a minimum of 1,600,000 vibrations per mono-second.... Energetically feel your resonance of gold-platinum light in the center of the vesica piscis, and command its 2 overlapping discs to spin.... Amplify your particle spin towards 1,700,000 vibrations, and feel your light accelerate throughout your circuit system....

In this moment, emanate the pulsations of these 2 templates throughout the central meridian of your spinal column, and then shift your awareness to the oversoul template....

While your consciousness is at the oversoul template, scan its circuitry, and feel your light within it.... With your crystalline hands implant the substance ether into the main power current of your spinal column.... Energetically feel your resonant pulsation of light as it flows through your circuitry....

Expand your light to encompass the oversoul template.... With your crystalline hands, energetically overlay its new configuration into your physiological circuitry, and through your fingertips, seal it with your resonance of gold-platinum light....

Feel your light spin your electron particles at a minimum of 1,700,000 vibrations.... Energetically feel your resonant pulsation of gold-platinum light in the center of the vesica piscis, and command its 2 overlapping discs to spin.... Amplify your electron particle spin towards 1,800,000 vibrations per mono-second, and feel your light accelerate throughout your circuit system....

Take a moment and synergize the frequency of this template throughout the main power current of your spinal column.... Be fully present with your experience, and when ready, shift your awareness to the christed-oversoul template....

Place your consciousness at the christed-oversoul template, and energetically feel your resonant pulsation of light within it.... Scan the circuitry of this template, and assimilate its new encodement.... With your crystalline hands implant the interstellar substance ether into the main power current of your spinal column.... Energetically overlay the new configuration for the christed-oversoul template into your physiological circuitry, and through your fingertips, seal it with gold-platinum light....

Feel your light spin your electron particles at a minimum of 1,800,000 vibrations per mono-second.... Energetically feel your resonance of gold-platinum light in the center of the vesica piscis, and command its 2 overlapping discs to spin.... Amplify your particle spin towards 1,900,000 vibrations, and feel your light accelerate throughout your circuit system....

In this moment, emanate the pulsation of this template throughout the central meridian of your spinal column, and then shift your awareness to the adam kadman template....

While your consciousness is at the adam kadmon template, scan its circuitry.... Energetically feel your light as the epitome of perfection, adam kadmon elohim, in human embodiment.... With your crystalline hands implant the substance ether into the main power current of your spinal column....

Expand your light to encompass this template.... With your crystalline hands, energetically overlay its new configuration into your physiological circuitry, and through your fingertips, seal it with your light....

Feel your light spin your electron particles at a minimum of 1,900,000 vibrations.... Energetically feel your resonant pulsation of gold-platinum light in the center of the vesica piscis, and command its 2 overlapping discs to spin.... Amplify your electron particle spin towards 2,000,000 vibrations per mono-second, and feel your light accelerate throughout your circuit system....

Take a moment and synergize the frequency of this template throughout the main power current of your spinal column.... Be fully present with your experience, and when ready, shift your awareness to the zohar and gematrian templates....

Place your consciousness at the zohar template, scan its circuitry, and energetically feel your resonance of light within it.... Shift your awareness to the gematrian template, and scan the circuitry of this template.... Energetically feel your own resonant pulsation of light as shekinah, and emanate it throughout your circuit system.... With your crystalline hands implant the interstellar substance ether into the main power current of your spinal column.... Energetically overlay the new configuration for these 2 templates into your physiological circuitry, and through your fingertips, seal each one with your resonance of gold-platinum light....

Feel your light spin your electron particles at a minimum of 2,000,000 vibrations per mono-second.... Energetically feel your resonant pulsation of gold-platinum light in the center of the vesica piscis, and command its 2 overlapping discs to spin.... Further amplify your particle spin towards 2,300,000 vibrations, and feel your light accelerate throughout your circuit system.... In this moment, emanate the pulsations of these 2 templates throughout the central meridian of your spinal column, and be fully present with your experience....

Shift your awareness to the center of the earth-star, and feel your light within it.... Energetically feel your light within this unified configuration and ground into your physiological circuitry....

When ready, bring your awareness to where you are in the moment, and breathe into your experience.

✡   ✡   ✡

For those of us who need to see our interdimensional forms,
there is universal sadness.
For those of us who align with intergalactic transmissions,
there is the embrace of galactic family.
Yet, for those of us who claim our consciousness
while in human embodiment,
...welcome home.

Consciousness on the New Earth

Paradise on the New Earth

The lost continent of lemuria comprises an advanced state of awareness that emanates multidimensional intelligence and knowledge. Through our own resonance of light in lemuria, we remember this awareness and integrate it into the present moment. Therefore, the more we enable these memories to surface and reveal what life is like more than 30,000 years ago, the more we receive an encodement of essential information. This encodement inaugurates the return of paradise on earth, which assists us in creating a thriving society in the new matrix of life.

The way we choose to experience our paradise depends on our willingness to accept all that we are as unified consciousness, and bring this awareness home so that it resides in our hearts.

Life on the new earth supports the consciousness of inner communion; we work together in a unified time-space continuum that is virtually comprised of no-time and no-space. We experience paradise on the new earth through our willingness to live in harmony and equality with ourselves and other life forms.

Our Consciousness as Cosmic Emissaries of Light

Consciousness is unified and eternal, and we energetically feel the synergy of our light, *adonai elohim adonai* [ah-do-nigh' e-lo-heem' ah-do-nigh'], through the brotherhood of light, *melek b'nai or*. The frequency of light within this indefinable vastness pulsates throughout infinity, and as we naturally synergize our own resonance of cosmic intelligence we experience inner communion with all that we are.

Through the synergy of advanced technology we transmit a beacon of light that is received by our own resonance of this intelligence within the 6th, 7th, 8th and 9th dimensional planes of awareness. Therefore, as long as we maintain our alignment, our consciousness returns the transmission to wherever we are on earth.

Everything that is unconscious becomes conscious and we formulate a co-creative partnership with self in service to the divine plan. We are emissaries of light such as; chohans, archangels, seraphim and cherubim, elohim, intergalactic federation, record keepers, planetary logos, solar logos, kuchavim, starseeds, and so on.

The information in this chapter is a minimal overview of this co-creative partnership, and merely opens the portal to adjust to this valid concept. As you read this chapter and energetically feel the frequency of its keys, you may feel ungrounded, and out of your body. The more you pay attention to body sensations, such as; inner visions, communication through inner hearing, or the innate sensation of vibrational frequencies, the more you receive energetic transmissions directly from all that you are as unified consciousness.

As unified consciousness you know how to live in divinity, which is essential to life on the new earth. Are you ready to knowingly interact with the vastness of all that you are?

Our Consciousness as Chohans

As chohans, we transmit the full spectrum of light within the first 7 rays that permeate earth. Through our synthesis of these rays, we assimilate many frequencies of light and pass through 4 phases of ascension that range from awakening to mastery. As this cosmic emissary of light, we neutralize all polarization and facilitate in the transformation of global situations, so that they are in accordance with the divine plan.

As Archangels, We Are the Tree of Life

For eons many spiritual traditions reference the angelic realm and its archangels as external sources of light, yet our full embodiment as this consciousness is an energetic bridge to the lineage of our intergalactic origin. The only road map that directs us to this innate knowing is the one that we create for ourselves, and through devotion and commitment to our spiritual graduation we receive advanced spiritual perspectives and understandings.

Our resonance of light, as archangels, sustains the wisdom that emanates from the sefirot of the *esh ka eem*, the kabbalistic tree of life. This tree of unified consciousness sustains advanced angelic intelligence, which derives from the zohar, a text of kabbalistic wisdom. This wisdom assimilates into our awareness through the mystical kabbalistic sefirot, which the phoenician archives reveal dates back to 1300 b.c.

This kabbalistic tree sustains 3 triads of unified awareness: triad of the masculine principle, triad of feminine principle and the triad of balance. The culmination of all 3 sustains 10 branches of unified consciousness that synergize distinct characteristics of divine will. Conscious awareness of all that we are within the tree of life primes us for complete transfiguration of traditional kabbalistic wisdom.

Inner communion with our angelic light requires that we claim our divine birthright, energetically feel our light in each sefirah, regulate all cosmic portals in earth's galaxy and transfigure dissonant energies before they enter earth's atmosphere. As archangels, we also preserve spiritual texts, restructure spiritual teachings in specific traditions and facilitate evolution on earth.

The illustration for *Resonance of Light in the Angelic Tree of Life* shows the traditional kabbalistic model, however it omits the interstellar organization of 3 sefirahs, which are deliberately withheld to keep our consciousness in limitation. These 3 sefirahs are outlined and assimilated in the next chapter, in the chart *Interstellar Sefirot of Earth's Galaxy* and the key that accompanies it.

The following overview and illustration for the tree of life reveals all that we are as angelic emissaries of light:

> At the top of the triad of balance is the sefirah kether, which emanates our light, as metatron. As this angelic emissary of light, we are clothed in the garment of el shaddai and emanate conscious divinity in its purest form;

> The sefirah at the top of the masculine triad is chochmah and sustains our resonance of light as ratziel. Through this sefirah we experience evolution as it is within the divine plan;

> At the top of the feminine triad is the sefirah binah, which emanates our light, as tzaphkiel. As this angelic emissary of light, we emanate cosmic pulsations throughout the subtle circuit system;

> The middle sefirah of the masculine triad is chesed and sustains our resonance of light as tzadkiel. Through this sefirah we transfigure energetic distortion into perfection;

> In the middle of the feminine triad is the sefirah geburah, which emanates our light as khamael. As this angelic emissary of light, we radiate cosmic intelligence throughout consciousness;

> The upper middle sefirah in the triad of balance is tiphereth and sustains our resonance of light as mikael. Through this sefirah we embody the crown of immortality, and this galactic coronation enables us to experience our divine birthright;

> At the bottom of the masculine triad is the sefirah netzach, which emanates our light, as auriel. As this angelic emissary of light, we

radiate cosmic order and synergy throughout consciousness;

The sefirah at the bottom of the feminine triad is hod and sustains our resonance of light, as raphael. Through this sefirah we emanate divinity;

The lower middle sefirah in the triad of balance is yesod, which emanates our light, as gabriel. As this angelic emissary of light, we emit cosmic wisdom, share knowledge on the circles of unity, and fulfill divine service;

The sefirah at the bottom of the triad of balance is malkuth and sustains our resonance of light, as sandalphon. Through this sefirah we synergize earth's new blueprint into our circuit system. We energetically feel our own resonant pulsation of light within all 10 sefirahs and consciously know how to live as angelic light on the new earth.

Resonance of Light in the Angelic Tree of Life

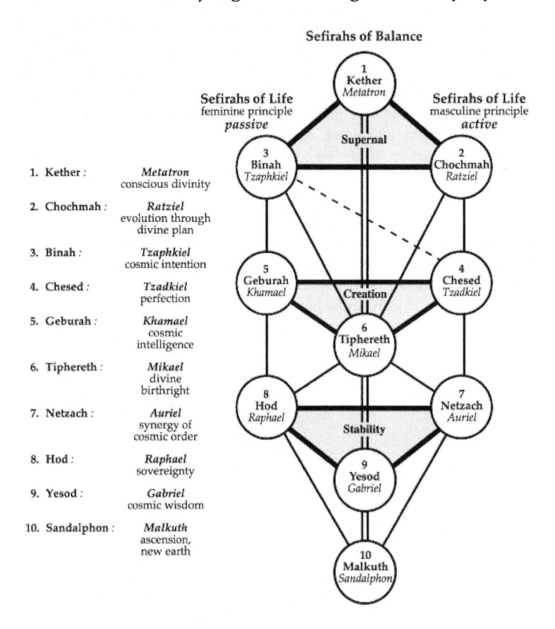

1. Kether :   *Metatron*
                   conscious divinity

2. Chochmah :   *Ratziel*
                   evolution through
                   divine plan

3. Binah :   *Tzaphkiel*
                   cosmic intention

4. Chesed :   *Tzadkiel*
                   perfection

5. Geburah :   *Khamael*
                   cosmic
                   intelligence

6. Tiphereth :   *Mikael*
                   divine
                   birthright

7. Netzach :   *Auriel*
                   synergy of
                   cosmic order

8. Hod :   *Raphael*
                   sovereignty

9. Yesod :   *Gabriel*
                   cosmic wisdom

10. Sandalphon :   *Malkuth*
                    ascension,
                    new earth

Sefirahs of Balance

Sefirahs of Life
feminine principle
passive

Sefirahs of Life
masculine principle
active

1
Kether
Metatron

Supernal

3
Binah
Tzaphkiel

2
Chochmah
Ratziel

5
Geburah
Khamael

Creation

4
Chesed
Tzadkiel

6
Tiphereth
Mikael

8
Hod
Raphael

7
Netzach
Auriel

Stability

9
Yesod
Gabriel

10
Malkuth
Sandalphon

Key: Experience Your Resonance of Light, as Archangels

In this key, you energetically synthesize your own resonance of angelic light into the main power current of your spinal column.

Allow your inner guidance to direct the pace of this assimilation, as you may find it necessary to experience one section of this key at a time. If so, ground your energy in the center of the earth-star, and resume with the next section, when appropriate.

Throughout this key your light spins your electron particles at a minimum of 2,300,000 vibrations per mono-second. Observe the illustration on the previous page for the directional flow of this key before you begin.

✿　✿　✿

With great reverence, energetically feel the cosmic cadence of the solar heart, as your pulsating rhythm.... Intuitively sense your light within the tree of life, and breathe into your own resonance of angelic frequency....

Shift your awareness to the sefirah at the top of the triad of balance, and energetically feel your light within kether.... As the angelic emissary of light metatron, emanate the angelic garment of el shaddai, and experience conscious divinity as it assimilates into the main power current of your spinal column....

Energetically feel your frequency as it flows through the interconnecting circuitry, diagonally downward to the top of the masculine triad.... While your consciousness is in this sefirah, feel your light within chochmah.... As the emissary ratziel, transcend the imperfect conditions of human life, and experience evolution through the divine plan....

Intuitively sense your frequency, within the interconnecting circuitry, as it flows across to the top of the feminine triad.... Shift your awareness to the sefirah, binah, and feel your angelic light within it.... As the archangel tzaphkiel, emanate pulsations of cosmic intention throughout your circuitry....

Energetically feel your resonance of light as archangels metatron, ratziel and tzaphkiel, and assimilate it into the main power current of your spinal column.... With absolute certainty, declare the following spoken word:

> "As the light within the sefirah kether,
> *I AM* the angelic emissary, metatron.
> In the sefirah chochmah,
> *I AM* the emissary, ratziel.
> As the light in binah,
> *I AM* archangel tzaphkiel."

In this moment, be fully present with your experience.... Then, sense your frequency as it flows through the interconnecting circuitry, diagonally downward to the sefirah in the middle of the masculine triad....

✡

While your consciousness is in the sefirah in the middle of the masculine triad, energetically feel your light within chesed.... As the emissary tzadkiel, transfigure distortion into perfection....

Intuitively sense your frequency as it flows through the interconnecting circuitry, across to the sefirah in the middle of the feminine triad.... Shift your awareness to the sefirah, geburah, and energetically feel your light within it.... As the angelic emissary of light khamael, emanate cosmic intelligence throughout consciousness....

Sense your frequency within the interconnecting circuitry, as it flows diagonally downward to the upper middle sefirah in the triad of balance.... While your consciousness is in the sefirah, tiphereth, feel your light.... As archangel mikael, experience immortality through your galactic coronation, and experience your divine birthright....

Energetically feel your resonance of light as archangels tzadkiel, khamael and mikael, and assimilate it into the main power current of your spinal column.... Through conscious intention and with absolute certainty, declare the following spoken word:

"As the light within the sefirah chesed,
I AM the emissary tzadkiel.
In the sefirah geburah,
I AM the angelic emissary of light, khamael.
As the light in tiphereth,
I AM archangel mikael."

Take a moment and be fully present with your experience.... Then, sense your frequency, as it flows through the interconnecting circuitry, diagonally downward to the sefirah at the bottom of the masculine triad....

✡

While your consciousness is in the sefirah at the bottom of the masculine triad, energetically feel your light in netzach.... As the angelic emissary of light auriel, emanate cosmic order and synergy throughout consciousness....

Intuitively sense your frequency, as it flows through the interconnecting circuitry, across to the sefirah at the bottom of the feminine triad.... Shift your awareness to hod, and as the emissary raphael, emanate divinity....

Sense your frequency within the interconnecting circuitry, as it flows diagonally downward to the lower middle sefirah in the triad of balance.... While your consciousness is in yesod, as archangel gabriel, transmit cosmic wisdom through unity, love and service....

Energetically feel your resonance of light as archangels auriel, raphael and gabriel, and assimilate it into the main power current of your spinal column.... Through your intention and with absolute certainty, declare the following spoken word:

> "As the light within the sefirah netzach,
> *I AM* the angelic emissary, auriel.
> In the sefirah hod,
> *I AM* the emissary, raphael.
> "As the light in yesod,
> *I AM* archangel gabriel."

In this moment, be fully present with your experience.... Then, sense your frequency, as it flows through the interconnecting circuitry, downward to the sefirah at the bottom of the triad of balance....

While your consciousness is in the sefirah at the bottom of the triad of balance, energetically feel your light within malkuth.... As the angelic emissary of light, sandalphon, consciously assimilate the cosmic cadence of the new earth.... Through conscious intention, declare the following spoken word:

"As the angelic emissary of light within malkuth,
I AM sandalphon, and
support the foundation for unified consciousness
on the new earth."

Feel your light spin your electron particles at a minimum of 2,300,000 vibrations.... Emanate your own resonant pulsation of the 10 angelic frequencies in this sefirot throughout your circuit system.... Energetically feel your resonant pulsation of gold-platinum light in the center of the vesica piscis, and command its 2 overlapping discs to spin.... Amplify your electron particle spin towards 2,500,000 vibrations per mono-second, and feel this pulsation throughout your circuit system.... With absolute certainty, declare the following spoken word:

"As the unified angelic emissary of light,
I AM adam kadmon, the heavenly human, and
emanate the ineffable embodiment of creation,
ain soph or."

Shift your awareness to the center of the earth-star, and feel your light within it.... Energetically feel your light, as the embodiment of creation, and ground it into your physiological circuitry.... Feel your own resonance of the heavenly human on the new earth....

When ready, bring your awareness to where you are in the moment, and experience your angelic presence here on earth.

✿   ✿   ✿

Our Light as Seraphim and Cherubim

Through the highest order of angelic emissaries, as seraphim, we transmit the cosmic flame of infinite love throughout infinity. As cherubim, we record and translate thoughtforms that emanate directly from the seraphim.

As Elohim

Our consciousness as elohim guards an intergalactic portal between space and time, and governs our interstellar frequency of light as it emanates throughout all universes. Through divine grace we oversee cosmic law, emanate balance into duality and neutralize consciousness within planetary polarization.

Our Resonance of Light as the Intergalactic Federation

Our resonance of light as the intergalactic federation is part of a vast intelligent system of stellar organization. As consciousness within this federation we are a fleet of space commanders that oversee and govern all activities between interplanetary civilizations in this and other regions of distant universes. Our purpose is to uphold honor, integrity and equality among all life in all interplanetary civilizations, including that of the new earth. Like our consciousness on earth, we support the cosmic organization of united nations within the etheric realm to monitor all interactions that take place in other star systems, galaxies and universes.

We honor a doctrine of non-interference and work together as a unit to monitor and mediate interplanetary activities to assure peace and harmony throughout the cosmos. We maintain portals of light for all life forms to enter and exit from earth's star system as well as other star systems, galaxies and universes.

This intergalactic information is a stretch for many within mass consciousness, yet all that is required to transfigure any form of limitation is a shift in our perception, so that we open ourselves to receive the remembrance of all that we are, as a galactic citizen.

As Record Keepers

The more we realize that the full communion of our consciousness is but a moment away, the more we remember the true lineage of our intergalactic origin. As record keepers, we guard the knowledge of star systems and galaxies. In earth's star system we record the mythology of earth, which includes life on the continent mu, and the wisdom of its lemurian tablets and scrolls.

Resonance as Planetary Logos

As the resonance of planetary logos we hold the key to earth's quantum shift and synergize interstellar encodements into its grid. We synergize advanced technologies, scan potentialities and transfigure energy before it infiltrates and solidifies, so that it is compatible with earth's new atmosphere.

Our Resonance of Light as Solar Logos

Our resonance of light as solar logos fulfills the divine plan for earth's star system. It oversees all areas of cosmic governance, interprets energetic patterns from an intergalactic perspective and facilitates sovereignty on earth.

As Elders, We Are the Kuchavim

As we cross another interstellar threshold, our consciousness as the *kuchavim* [ku-cha'-vim], or council of 12 in the star system sirius, is in full communion with our twin ray on the council of 24 elders. We are 12 sets of galactic twin-flames that administer cosmic order as directed by our consciousness as ain soph or.

Our Frequency as Starseeds

As starseeds, we journey throughout many universes, synergize the dna of each root race, germinate an intergalactic seed within human consciousness and birth into individualized form. Our intergalactic presence actively seeds another genesis, as we emanate cosmic transmissions to and from civilizations light years away.

As embodied starseeds living on earth, we are in service to the divine plan for the highest good of all. We facilitate awareness of intergalactic life and inject foreign concepts from this and other universes into earth's environment. We transfigure inadequate systems that are on the verge of evolutionary meltdown, align their construct to effectively download advanced technologies and implant them into the new systems established by lifestreams on the new earth.

As conscious starseeds, we offer a strong foothold for the synergy of cosmic intelligence—some of us administer our work silently, while others stand in the forefront. We interact with our consciousness as starseeds in other intergalactic civilizations, and assist one another so that we effectively facilitate humanity as it attains its full potential. We are open-hearted, yet many of us have a challenging time in our adjustment to human life, its materialistic density and the misinterpretation of free will. Yet, through our devotion and commitment to the divine plan we support human lifestreams as they become conscious of their own resonant pulsation of interstellar light.

Interstellar Encodement of the Galactic Lightbody

The new matrix of life requires that we synergize the interstellar encodement of the galactic lightbody into our circuit system. This encodement sustains a complex configuration of light that emanates as our own resonance of intergalactic intelligence attained through versatile experiences in other universes. When we are ready to synergize our resonance of this encodement, its interstellar frequency assimilates into our physiological circuitry at a *minimum* of 2,700,000 vibrations per mono-second.

The initial phase of the lightbody assimilation begins with synthesis of our light in the 9th ray, so that we are fully conscious of the subtle pulsations that occur within our physical body. The next phase synthesizes the 10th ray through which our resonance of light as oversoul anchors through the soul-star. It is through this ray that we remember lifetime upon lifetime of off-planet experiences. However, until we energetically feel our own resonance of light within the galactic lightbody, we experience a sense of disconnection from the true lineage of our intergalactic origin. As we remember our true lineage we feel safe in the physical body that we inhabit.

For those lifestreams currently in the integration of this experience, know that there are several steps to this progression. As the interstellar encodement of the galactic lightbody interpenetrates our circuit system, we experience an electric sensation throughout our physiological circuitry. This electrical current resembles tingling and numbness either in the extremities or throughout the whole body. Eventually this current settles and we energetically feel the essential resonance of light required to integrate it into our physiological circuitry, however, full synergy occurs on the new earth.

Once we adapt to the inclusiveness of the galactic lightbody, we earn our intergalactic passport; we are in divine service in accordance with the intended cosmic direction. In order to fulfill cosmic service, the lightbody transfigures its interstellar garment of light to suit the environment of the planets that it visits.

Key: Assimilate Your Resonance of the Galactic Lightbody

The more you assimilate your resonance of the galactic lightbody, the more you synergize its interstellar encodement throughout the main power current of your spinal column. As your physiological circuitry assimilates this encodement, you remember your intergalactic origin and bring this knowing into the present moment.

✧　✧　✧

With great reverence, energetically feel the cosmic cadence of the solar heart, as your pulsating rhythm.... While your consciousness is in this sacred space, energetically feel your own resonant frequency of the galactic lightbody surround your physical body.... With absolute certainty, set the intention to assimilate its interstellar encodement into your circuit system....

With your crystalline hands implant the substance ether into your solar heart, and emanate it throughout your physiological circuitry.... Shift your awareness to the palm of each hand, and energetically implant this interstellar substance into your hands.... Place your consciousness in the arch of each foot, and implant this ether into the circuitry of your feet.... When ready, energetically weave this interstellar substance between these 5 points in your body, and feel their cosmic pulsation throughout your circuitry....

Energetically overlay the lightbody encodement into your physical body, and through your fingertips, seal it with your own resonant pulsation of gold-platinum light.... In this moment, breathe your light into every area of your physical body, and be fully present with your experience....

Feel your light spin your electron particles at a minimum of 2,500,000 vibrations.... Energetically feel your own resonance of gold-platinum light in the center of the vesica piscis, and command its 2 overlapping discs to spin.... Amplify your electron particle spin towards 2,700,000 vibrations per mono-second, and feel your light accelerate throughout your circuit system....

Be fully present with your own resonant pulsation of the galactic lightbody.... Shift your awareness to the center of the earth-star, and feel your light within it.... Energetically feel your interstellar frequency ground into your physiological circuitry.... Take a moment, and breathe into your experience....

When ready, bring your awareness to where you are in the moment, breathe deeply, and energetically feel your full presence on the new earth.

✩   ✩   ✩

The galactic lightbody enables us to energetically project our consciousness throughout earth's star system, then go beyond its planets and explore other interplanetary civilizations beyond earth's galaxy. Begin this experiential journey with the next key.

Key: Lightbody Journey Throughout Earth's Star System

In this key your galactic lightbody supports your physical body while you energetically project your consciousness throughout earth's star system. As your frequency of light penetrates the interstellar field of 11 planets, you energetically feel your light within these interplanetary civilizations.

Allow your inner guidance to direct the pace of your cosmic journey, as you may find it necessary to experience one section of this key at a time. If so, ground your energy in the center of the earth-star, and resume your journey to the next star system, when appropriate. Enjoy the experience of your cosmic tour throughout earth's star system.

Throughout this key your light spins your electron particles at a minimum of 2,700,000 vibrations per mono-second.

✡   ✡   ✡

Place your consciousness in the center of the earth-star, and pull up your grounding cord from the center of this gateway.... Bring this cord upward through your spinal column to the solar heart, and energetically feel its cosmic cadence as your pulsating rhythm.

With grounding cord in hand, shift your awareness to the cosmic eye, and envision the configuration of earth's star system.... Project your awareness through a pillar of opalescent light, and energetically feel your own resonant frequency of the galactic lightbody.... Emanate this frequency into the configuration of earth's star system....

While your awareness is in the lightbody, travel to the cosmic force field of earth's sun.... Energetically feel your light in the interplanetary civilization of this cosmic star, and assimilate the energy from earth's sun into your circuit system.... Synergize this interstellar life force and breathe it into the main power current of your spinal column.... Through conscious intention and with absolute certainty, declare the following spoken word:

> "As a source of sun energy,
> *I AM* the light in earth's sun."

✡

Hold your grounding cord, as you consciously journey in your galactic lightbody to the force field of mercury, and feel your frequency of light emanate from this planet.... Intuitively sense your light in this interplanetary civilization, as it provides the opportunity for constant change in your life....

While your awareness is in the lightbody, continue your journey to the force field of venus, and intuitively sense your light in its civilization.... Synthesize infinite love and cosmic harmony as the purpose for life, and emanate this balance beyond this interplanetary civilization....

With grounding cord in hand, journey to earth's moon, and intuitively sense the light that emanates from it.... Feel your light in this interplanetary civilization as you harvest the wisdom of moon energy....

Energetically feel your own resonance of light embody in the planets mercury, venus and earth's moon.... Transmit your light to your circuit system, and with absolute certainty, declare the following spoken word:

"As constant change in earth's star system,
I AM the light in mercury.
As infinite love and cosmic harmony,
I AM a resonance of light within venus.
As the wisdom of moon energy,
I AM the light of the moon."

With grounding cord in hand, continue your journey to the cosmic force field of mars, and intuitively sense your light in its civilization.... Energetically feel the resonance of galactic self, and emanate your light beyond this interplanetary civilization....

While your awareness is in the galactic lightbody, journey to jupiter, and intuitively sense the light that emanates from this planet.... Synthesize your light in this interplanetary civilization....

Hold your grounding cord, as you consciously journey to the force field of saturn, and sense your light in its civilization.... Synergize your resonance of its interstellar light, and emanate it beyond this interplanetary civilization....

Energetically feel your resonant pulsation of light embody in the planets mars, jupiter and saturn.... When ready, transmit your light into the main power current of your spinal column.... Through conscious intention and absolute certainty, declare the following spoken word:

"As future self,
I AM a resonance of light within mars.
As the embodiment of vastness,
I AM the light in jupiter.
As the messenger for cosmic intelligence,
I AM light within saturn."

Hold your grounding cord, as you consciously journey in your galactic lightbody to the cosmic force field of uranus, and feel your resonant frequency of light emanate from this planet.... Intuitively sense your light in this interplanetary civilization as it innovates advanced energetic technology into your awareness....

While your awareness is in the lightbody, continue your journey to the force field of neptune, and intuitively sense your light in its civilization.... Give selfless service towards all lifestreams within this interplanetary civilization....

With grounding cord in hand, journey to pluto, and intuitively sense your resonant frequency of light that emanates from this planet.... Feel your light in this interplanetary civilization as it reinforces the unknown, and experience planetary transfiguration throughout your circuit system....

Energetically feel your resonance of light embody in the planets uranus, neptune and pluto.... Transmit your light to your circuit system, and with absolute certainty, declare the following spoken word:

> "As the bearer of advanced energetic technology,
> *I AM* the light in uranus.
> As devotion and selfless service,
> *I AM* a resonance of light within neptune.
> As the cosmic reinforcement
> for transfiguration into the unknown,
> *I AM* the light in pluto."

While your awareness is in the galactic lightbody, continue your journey to the cosmic force field of sedna.... Intuitively sense your light in this interplanetary civilization, and emanate your light beyond it.... With absolute certainty, declare the following spoken word:

> "As the union of all interplanetary civilizations,
> *I AM* a resonant pulsation of light within sedna."

Feel your light spin your electron particles at a minimum of 2,700,000 vibrations.... Energetically feel your resonance of light within the planet sedna, and assimilate it into the main power current of your spinal column.... Accept that your light emanates infinite love and cosmic union throughout earth's star system....

Energetically feel your own resonant frequency of gold-platinum light in the center of the vesica piscis, and command its 2 overlapping discs to spin.... Amplify your electron particle spin towards 3,000,000 vibrations per mono-second, and feel your light accelerate throughout your circuit system....

While your awareness is in the galactic lightbody, return to where you are on earth, and replace the grounding cord in the center of the earth-star.... Feel your resonant pulsation of light within it.... Energetically feel your light in 11 interplanetary civilizations fully manifest within your circuit system....

When ready, bring your awareness to where you are in the moment, and breathe into your experience.

✡ ✡ ✡

Yhsvh: Unified Consciousness of Yhvh and Shekinah

In the new matrix of life we live in full conscious divinity—a natural state of awareness in which we are whole and complete. Divinity sustains the pulsation of divine harmonics within the androgynous principles of yhvh and shekinah.

The tetragrammaton, 4-letter name, is considered by some lifestreams as the symbol for the ineffable name of god. It is comprised of 4 hebrew consonants that sustain hidden wisdom: *yod, heh, vahv* and *heh*. The yod symbolizes the androgynous principle of yhvh and its initial will of god; the first heh is the

176

symbol for the androgynous feminine principle *layooesh shekinah* [lay-oo-esh sh'ki nah]; the letter vahv symbolizes the contemplation of creation, while the second heh is the symbol for the communion of matter and spirit.

As the resonant pulsation of light within yhvh, we are the essence of all-that-is, which is demonstrated by jeshua through his actualized incarnation as god in human form. We are the androgynous masculine principle of ain living in 3rd dimensional reality, and as the resonance of light within shekinah, we are the androgynous feminine principle of soph; the unified seed of consciousness that nurtures the ultimate experience of inner communion. As we merge with our feminine principle, we open the energetic portal to our hidden mysteries, which takes us to the depth of our own abyss while in human embodiment. All the dark places buried deep within us rise to the surface, and when we are ready to let go, all of our doubts and fears dissolve. We consciously transfigure duality, balance polarization, and assimilate an authentic expression of strength, purity, conscious knowing and infinite love. And, as the androgynous principle of ain soph or we emanate this indwelling presence of divinity. Within this unified field of sovereignty we energetically feel the essence of all that we are, as yhsvh.

The pentagrammaton, yhsvh, is the divine blueprint of the tetragrammaton. Shin(s) denotes the totality of ain soph or, and when placed in the center of yhvh, it (yod, heh, *shin*, vahv, heh) symbolizes the process of creation, and consciousness comes full circle as divinity in human form. Therefore, the pentagrammaton symbolizes the physical union of the androgynous principles of yhvh and shekinah, as yhsvh. As we energetically feel this inner communion within our hearts, we experience the spiritual capstone to human life.

With absolute certainty, declare the following spoken word:

✿   ✿   ✿

"I AM yhsvh.
Androgyny is all things, seen and unseen,
here or there, neither here nor there."

✿   ✿   ✿

The Tetragrammaton

The Pentagrammaton

Androgynous Communion

Androgynous communion reveals that our own resonance of light within yhvh and shekinah pulsates to the harmonics of creation and emanates from within as yhsvh or ain soph or. As you experience inner communion, the masculine and feminine principles within you synergize their unified resonance of light into your heart.

During the experience of your graduation ceremony you are appropriately clothed, wearing a special etheric garment—a white robe with a personal insignia emblazoned in violet, gold and/or white that emanates the unified pulsation of your light. Throughout your ceremonial experience you energetically drink the interstellar elixir from your inner chalice of light.

Your graduation takes place through the interstellar matrix of your solar heart, and is energetically facilitated by the cosmic alignment of 2 grand trines: one ascending and the other descending. The fusion of these trines symbolize the configuration of the star of david, as the androgyny of ain soph or; this configuration of light is the synergy between the masculine principle yhvh, and the feminine principle, shekinah. As you consciously complete this interstellar fusion, you energetically feel the base of each trine bisect the 2 sides of the other trine. Your own resonance of light synergizes in the center of the star of david and emanates its cosmic harmony throughout infinity.

Complete synergy of this fusion reflects the essence of creation in human form. You hear the music of the celestial choir play the songs of the spheres and energetically feel its synchronistic rhythm emanate throughout the cosmos. Although your experience of this androgynous communion is unique to you, there is an energetic commonality—your union synchronizes the purpose of your human life, and you consciously emanate your essence as an experience of heaven on earth.

Star of David

Key: Experience Your Androgynous Communion

In this key you consciously experience the androgyny of inner communion. As you synergize your own resonance of light within the star of david, you energetically feel your essence, as yhsvh or ain soph or.

✿   ✿   ✿

With great reverence, energetically feel the cosmic cadence of the solar heart, as your pulsating rhythm.... Envision 2 grand trines, one as the ascending yhvh (ain) and the other as the descending shekinah (soph).... Place your consciousness in the center of the trine that is yhvh, and energetically feel your light.... Shift your awareness to the center of the trine that is shekinah, and energetically feel your own resonance of light....

With your crystalline hands implant the interstellar substance ether into the capstone of these trines, as they intersect with one another, to form a perfect geometric 6-pointed star.... Place your light in the center of this 6-pointed star, and overlay the star of david into your heart.... Through your fingertips seal the overlay with your own resonance of gold-platinum light.... Energetically feel the cadence of your cosmic rhythm, as it pulsates within you.... In this moment, be fully present with your experience, and feel great reverence in your heart for your own unified frequency of light....

Feel your light spin your electron particles at a minimum of 3,000,000 vibrations.... Energetically feel your resonant pulsation of gold-platinum light in the center of the vesica piscis, and command its 2 overlapping discs to spin.... Amplify your electron particle spin towards 3,500,000 vibrations per mono-second, and feel your light accelerate throughout your circuit system....

As the unified consciousness of yhsvh or ain soph or, give voice to your divinity.... With absolute certainty, declare the following spoken word:

181

Yhsvh
I AM ain
I AM the consciousness of ain soph or
I AM yhvh
I AM in full divinity
I AM that *I AM*
I AM light
I AM that *I AM*
I AM in full divinity
I AM shekinah
I AM the consciousness of ain soph or
I AM soph
Yhsvh

Shift your awareness to the center of the earth-star, and feel your light within it.... Energetically feel your resonant pulsation of unified light ground into your physiological circuitry through the main power current of your spinal column....

When ready, bring your awareness to where you are in the moment, and breathe into your experience.

✿　✿　✿

Interstellar Frequency of the Cosmic Cross

The sacred symbol of the cosmic cross radiates vertical and horizontal frequencies, which emanate as our interstellar resonance of light within the galactic core.

Its formation comprises 2 lines, one vertical and the other horizontal. When one line is placed on top of the other, in equal proportion, the symbol forms 4 branches that intersect in the middle.

This interstellar symbol radiates specific fusion within earth's elements: fire, water, air, earth and ether. The original 4 platonic solids: hexahedron, tetrahedron, octahedron, and dodecahedron maintain their form, yet merge as the 5th dimensional icosa-dodecahedron, which comprises the interstellar substance ether. The neutron, duatron and photon merge and create the electron, which is adhesive energy; therefore, the unified frequency in the center of the cosmic cross reflects the sum is now greater than its original components.

The more we synergize our own resonant pulsation of light in the cosmic cross, the more we experience greater equilibrium in our day-to-day life.

Key: Synergize Your Light in the Cosmic Cross

In this key you synergize your light with the resonant pulsation of the cosmic cross, and energetically feel the equilibrium that emanates from the center of its vertical and horizontal frequencies....

✿   ✿   ✿

Energetically feel the cosmic cadence of the solar heart, as your pulsating rhythm.... Shift your awareness to the central point of this interstellar symbol, and energetically feel your own resonance of light within it....

While your awareness is in the center of this symbol, energetically feel its adhesive energy.... With your crystalline hands overlay this interstellar configuration at the cosmic eye in the center of your forehead, and through your fingertips, seal the overlay with your resonance of gold-platinum light....

When ready, shift your awareness to your physical body.... Energetically feel your resonance of the cosmic cross as you place it to the left and right of you, behind and in front, above and below you and in the center of the solar heart.... In this moment, be fully present with your experience....

Energetically feel your resonant pulsation of gold-platinum light spin your electron particles at a minimum of 3,500,000 vibrations per mono-second, and feel this pulsation in the main power current of your spinal column....

Shift your awareness to the center of the earth-star, and feel your light within it.... Energetically feel your resonant pulsation of light within the cosmic cross ground into your physiological circuitry....

When ready, bring your awareness to where you are in the moment, and breathe into your experience.

✿   ✿   ✿

Configuration of Light in the Cosmic Cross

Within the cosmos
the new earth illuminates the heavens
as a star.

New Encodement Within the Heavens

New Configurations in Astronomy

As we experience the momentum of the quantum shift earth experiences consecration of its waters, air and soil. Land masses shift—some of which rise from the waters and others return to the waters. Many lifestreams make their transition from earth during this time, whereas others experience mass migration to other locations.

As earth shifts into its destined alignment within the cosmos it receives its new encodements through a series of geometric configurations. Although the full encodement within these configurations is veiled from our awareness, their resonant pulsations of light catapult all the planets in earth's star system to their next level of evolution. This is the tipping point at which a new galaxy forms and earth transfigures into its perfect heavenly form—a star.

There are a number of major astronomy configurations that occur between august 1999 and 2012 that reinforce the significance of earth's quantum shift into its stellar blueprint. In the moment of this writing, some of the preliminary configurations are:

Grand Cross of Earth's Star System

In august 1999 a cosmic event facilitates a new encodement within the heavens as earth aligns with the planets in its star system. With the exception of pluto, all the planets in our star system, plus 3 asteroids, align with taurus, leo, scorpio or aquarius. This forms a grand cross where all of the planets either conjunct, square or oppose one another.

Jupiter and saturn align in the fixed earth sign taurus. The sun, mercury, venus, the asteroid ceres, as well as the north node of the moon are in the fixed fire sign leo. In the fixed water sign scorpio, the moon, mars, and the asteroids chiron and juno conjunct. Neptune, uranus and the south node of the moon are in the fixed air sign aquarius. Together these planets form a grand cross of light that opens a cosmic stargate to the 7th golden age. This cosmic configuration reflects the completion of earth's karmic cycles.

Star of David Configuration

The 2nd significant heavenly event occurs in the linear year 2003 and creates a new planetary configuration, which activates an interdimensional stargate in earth's star system. This is the 1st time in human history that this specific configuration sustains a tachyon particle field that emanates light throughout the cosmos.

This event is actually comprised of 2 simultaneous events—a total lunar eclipse along with a grand sextile. The energies of this total lunar eclipse synergize with the frequencies of 6 planets in earth's star system. The planets mars, saturn and the sun form a cosmic triangle known as a grand trine. The moon, jupiter and the asteroid chiron form the other grand trine and together both trines create the 6-pointed star of david. The rare encodement in this heavenly configuration heralds the androgynous communion of yhvh and shekinah within us.

Stellar Activation of Venus Transits

In 2004, venus eclipses the sun and the stellar activation of this transit facilitates a breakthrough in our consciousness. The linear timeframe between this transit and the next venus eclipse of the sun in 2012 inaugurates earth's final moment of truth. In 2012 all stargates are open and the energetic current of transfiguration is in full force in earth's star system.

As the planet venus passes across the sun for 7 hours during the transit of june 6, 2012, this cosmic event emanates the final energetic capstone for human life. The stellar stargate for the 7th golden age closes on this date and inaugurates the quantum shift into life on the new earth. If we ignore the opportunity to assimilate the frequencies within these 2 transits, we deny ourselves the right to experience multidimensional awareness.

Pluto Conjuncts the Galactic Core

In the linear time between these 2 venus transits, pluto makes a rare conjunction to the galactic core in 2006 and 2007. This is the first time that this configuration is conscious in our awareness, as during previous occurrences, pluto and its influences extend beyond the realm of our perception.

Over the course of this 2-year period other planetary bodies contribute to this celestial dynamic and add to the synergy of this cosmic event. As pluto marks its final conjunction beyond the galactic core, it aligns with jupiter, earth's sun and mercury. It emanates a momentum of profound transformation, transfiguration, intergalactic communication and inner communion throughout consciousness. This 2-year long conjunction of quaking at the deepest core of our being reflects attributes that we have yet to access. Long associated with transformation and transfiguration, death and rebirth, this momentous plutonian alignment emerges as death of the known and birth of the unknown.

Massive Stellar Explosion

In september 2006, scientists detect an extremely rare stellar explosion in a galaxy 240 million light years away, called ngc1260. This explosion is fueled by antimatter and is 100 times more energetic than typical supernovas. Scientists determine that this supernova, which they name sn2006gy, is evidence of a newly discovered category.

Supernovas contain a star with 8-20 times the mass of our sun, which collapses under its own gravity. Super massive stars produce an abundance of gamma-ray light that converts into matter and anti-matter, which comprises mostly electrons and positrons. A particle of anti-matter and a particle of matter have the same mass yet, its atomic properties such as its charge and the direction of its spin are opposite.

This discovery denotes the chain reaction of transfiguration in this universe. As earth shifts into its rightful position in the cosmos, a domino effect occurs throughout all star systems, galaxies and universes. Everything in creation shifts into its next phase of evolution.

Stellar Alignment of Venus and Pleiades

The alignment between venus and pleiades on july 7, 2007 is a stellar occurrence that prepares us for the grand opening of the sirius stargate. As this stargate opens, its frequency emanates a new encodement of light and inserts it into the planetary grid.

This energetic alignment reflects the cosmic symbology of triple 7 for heightened spirituality and advanced technology, which enables multiple stellar frequencies of light to amplify our spiritual awareness 3-fold.

As the collective momentum of these configurations impact us, we are in perfect cosmic alignment for a life of multidimensional awareness, and we refine all of our contracts so that new agreements come into play.

Configuration of Major Stargates

In the heavens 2 major stargates open before the end of the year 2007, and, both of these stargates reinforce the significance of a new configuration within the cosmos. The frequency of the 1ˢᵗ stargate synergizes a new set of interstellar codes in the grid system, which indicates that we are in an advanced phase of evolution. The 2ⁿᵈ stargate activates the final encodement within those lifestreams who contract to assist others in the new matrix of life.

Our innate ability to synergize the frequencies that radiate from these 2 stargates depends on how we experience the forward momentum into the new matrix of life.

Interstellar Sefirot of Earth's Galaxy

Star systems are groupings of stars, planets, moons and other cosmic phenomena that orbit within a gravitational force field of cosmic energy. The interplanetary civilizations in these star systems are influenced by the stars' cosmic essence, and our resonant pulsation of light within these systems absorbs the attributes of that essence.

The interstellar sefirot of earth's galaxy is the spiritual vessel of infinite light that bridges our consciousness with other star systems in earth's galaxy. In the traditional kabbalistic tree of life, the center pillar of mysticism comprises only 4 sefirahs, yet in the interstellar sefirot of earth's galaxy, the unified tree of life synergizes 3 additional sefirahs. These sefirahs sustain encodements from 3 other star systems, which complete the missing links to our consciousness.

This unified sefirot comprises 12 star systems: the new earth, earth's sun, etheric feminine sun, midway station, etheric masculine sun, pleiades, antares, arcturus, sirius, alpha, galactic core and omega. As we synergize our light within each of these star systems, we expand our consciousness into the 13ᵗʰ star system, omnigalactic source. This system is also known as ain soph or, which oversees everything as whole and complete. Through the synergy of this star system we experience the nothing and everything simultaneously. While in this place of cosmic balance we claim our galactic origin and experience our divine birthright as intergalactic citizens.

Following is a general overview of the interstellar sefirot of earth's galaxy:

New earth—orbits around its sun(s) at a distance of approximately 93 million miles or 150 million kilometers.

As earth charts its new course through the heavens, its revolution increases in momentum and this acceleration synergizes a new grid system that fully transfigures the frequency of light in its ley lines and vortices. In the moment of earth's quantum shift, many of these ley lines and vortices completely transfigure; therefore, this modification creates another grid system that fully supports the new earth.

The interstellar matrix of hues for the new earth swirls inside a spiral of radiant iridescent hues of vibrant gold, platinum, violet, cobalt blue, emerald green, yellow and pink.

Earth's sun—is a step-down transformer for the galactic core. It receives energy directly from this star system, and emanates increasing cosmic pulsations that interpenetrate many celestial systems. As a conduit for transmissions from the galactic core, the frequencies in earth's sun filter through earth's grid and permeate our circuit system;

Androgynous feminine sun—as our own resonant frequency of this consciousness, we emanate the feminine attribute of infinite love;

Midway station—is a cosmic stopover point where we integrate our remembrance from other interplanetary timelines;

Androgynous masculine sun—as our own resonant frequency of this awareness, we emanate the masculine attribute of infinite love;

Pleiades—from the perspective of earth, pleiades is in the constellation eta tauri, also known as taurus. This system contains mostly hot blue stars, is 400 light years from earth and is the most visible star system in earth's galaxy. It contains clusters of hundreds of stars, some of which are visible to our naked eye from where we are on earth, including alcyone, electra, merope, asterope, taygeta, celaeno, maia, pleione and atlas.

Alcyone is the central sun of this star system and is 1,000 times more luminous than earth's sun. As the resonance of light within alcyone, we facilitate in the energetic transmission of cosmic intelligence from other interplanetary civilizations. And, we enhance our innate ability to perceive life in other star systems as well as in other galaxies and universes. In electra our light oversees the way we receive its intergalactic transmissions, and the rest of the stars in this system synergize our consciousness with their stellar frequencies of light.

Our resonant pulsation of light within all the stars in pleiades communicates through thought;

Antares—the distance from earth to antares is 520 - 600 light years and is in alpha scorpii, also known as the constellation scorpio. It is a variable red super giant star that is 12,000 times brighter than earth's sun.

There are 2 planets equidistant from antares that emanates the polarization of light and dark. Our resonance of light in antares supports a planet that emanates infinite love and another planet that denies infinite love. Life on antares offers an experiential understanding of how both planets bring the polarization of light and dark into balance;

Arcturus—from the perspective of earth, arcturus is 36.7 light years away, and its bright star is in the constellation alpha bootis. It is a yellow giant star and the 4th brightest star in earth's sky. Its diameter is 18 times the diameter of earth's sun and 4 times its mass. It is 105 times as luminous as earth's sun, yet the temperature is 1,500 degrees lower because of its greater surface size.

Formed in the halo of the milky way, there is a cosmic portal into this star system, which is an entry and exit point for space travel beyond this galaxy. This star system also serves as another stopover point that guides cosmic travel within earth's galaxy.

Arcturus inhabits one of the most advanced interplanetary civilizations in earth's galaxy. The civilizations of arcturians emanate interstellar knowledge from several of its planets, yet as a whole the wisdom that radiates from this star system influences the entire galaxy.

Our resonant pulsation of consciousness in arcturus guards archives, which contain key documents on intergalactic principles, and govern intelligence in other interplanetary civilizations. It also records codes of light directly from the sun of arcturus. The true nature of how we use these codes energetically transfigures one frequency of light into another. As an inhabitant of arcturus, we earn our intergalactic passport for travel beyond earth's galaxy;

Sirius—is 8.7 million light years from earth. This bright star system is in the constellation alpha canis majoris, the larger of orion's 2 hunting dogs. It is a binary system of stars, sirius-a plus sirius-b. Both stars emit frequencies that seed the characteristics of transfiguration.

Sirius-a, a blue-white dwarf star, is rich in elements heavier than hydrogen. It is 23 times brighter than earth's sun and twice its size. Sirius-b is a white dwarf star, one percent of the size of earth's sun, and nears the end of its life as it runs out of hydrogen, its stellar fuel.

The stars in this binary system are in close proximity, with only 20 times the distance of earth to its sun. The point of their closest approach to one another varies throughout their orbits. This cosmic interaction causes transfiguration in the magnetic fields of this binary system, and shifts the axis and orbit for all of the planets that cycle around sirius-a and b.

Sirius directly affects earth's quantum shift; this star system supports us as we restore our dna into its original configuration of energy and synergize it within our physiological circuitry.

Alpha—is the androgynous principle of an endless boundless presence, ain soph, and with its complement omega, both are the highest expression of twin-ray emanations in earth's galaxy. Our resonance of light in alpha is the in-breath of creation and transfigures the paradigm of duality on earth;

Galactic core—is 26,000 light years from earth's sun and sustains huge clouds of interstellar gases that birth stars as frequencies of light. The galactic core is part of a cosmic orb over 2 million times the mass of earth's sun, and it emanates approximately 20 million times as much energy.

Frequencies of light within the galactic core are invisible to the naked eye, yet transmit cosmic radiance through a grid of geometric codes. Our resonance of light in the galactic core synergizes the interstellar frequency of the cosmic cross and emanates it beyond the star systems in earth's galaxy;

Omega—is the twin-ray and androgynous complement to alpha. Our resonance of light in omega is the out-breath of creation and emanates the full cycle of life. As the frequency of omega, we transfigure duality and experience the nothing and everything simultaneously;

Omnigalactic source—unifies the interstellar sefirot of earth's galaxy. Our resonance of light in this star system, dematerializes, bi-locates to other planets, and if necessary, rematerializes in the form that suits the individual planet within the star system of that galaxy. As the resonant pulsation of omnigalactic source we are whole and complete, as ain soph or.

Our light, as ain soph or, is the infusion of consciousness and light within every star system, galaxy and universe. We experience ain, the void before creation; ain soph, as infinite space, and ain soph or, as creation.

In the following illustration observe 3 additional sefirahs in the triad of balance that complete the missing links in consciousness.

Interstellar Sefirot of Earth's Galaxy

Omnigalactic Source :	13th Dimension
Omega :	Out-breath of Creation
Galactic Core :	Interstellar Grid of Geometric Codes
Alpha :	In-breath of Creation
Sirius :	Activates Original Configuration of DNA
Arcturus :	Monitors Encodements of Light
Antares :	Cosmic Synergy
Pleiades :	Telepathic Communication
Androgynous Masculine Sun :	Activation
Midway Station :	Balance
Androgynous Feminine Sun :	Receptivity
Earth's Sun :	Celestial Conduit
New Earth :	Crystalline Form

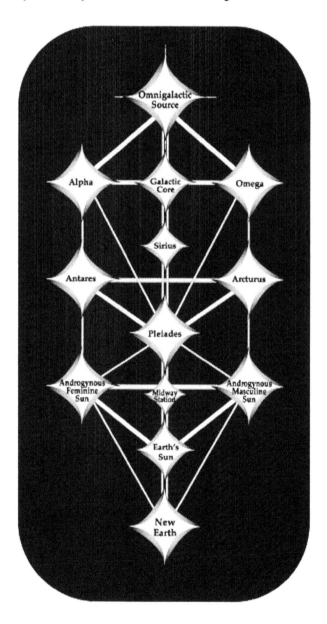

Key: Synergize the Interstellar Encodement for Earth's Galaxy

In this key the galactic lightbody supports your physical body as your consciousness weaves its light through the star systems to the 13th sefirah in earth's galaxy.

As in previous keys, your crystalline hands implant the substance ether into your circuit system, energetically overlay the interstellar encodement of each star system, and seal it with your own resonance of gold-platinum light. Once full assimilation for all the systems is complete you energetically sense the pulsations of 3 additional systems to the missing links in consciousness; you feel your own resonant pulsation of light as omnigalactic source.

Due to the encodement of light in this key, it is suggested that you read it several times to familiarize yourself with its substance, and only when you feel you are ready, overlay each encodement as your inner guidance directs you. This prevents energetic overload as well as excessive overwhelm.

If in any moment you require extra time to synergize this encodement, ground your energy in the center of the earth-star. Resume with the next star system, when appropriate. Be fully present with the sensations that arise in your physical body and remember complete synergy occurs in its own time.

Throughout this key your light naturally spins your electron particles at a minimum of 3,500,000 vibrations per mono-second. Before you begin, observe the accompanying illustration for navigational direction, then enjoy the journey.

✡　✡　✡

Energetically feel the cosmic cadence of the solar heart, as your pulsating rhythm.... Envision the interstellar sefirot of earth's galaxy, and place your consciousness within its configuration of star systems.

✡

Shift your awareness to the earth-star, and take hold of your grounding cord at its center.... Energetically feel your resonant frequency of light in the center of the earth, and synergize its magnetic energy throughout your circuit system....

Hold your grounding cord, and consciously journey in your lightbody to earth's sun, the star system just above the new earth at the bottom of the triad of balance.... Energetically feel your light in this system as it activates your cosmic fire in the galactic core.... With your crystalline hands implant the interstellar substance ether into your circuit system, and overlay its encodement into the main power current of your spinal column.... Through your fingertips, seal this encodement with your resonance of gold-platinum light....

Take a moment, and be fully present with your light as it emanates from the new earth and its sun(s), then continue your journey to the androgynous feminine sun....

With grounding cord in hand, journey in your galactic lightbody to the androgynous feminine sun, the star system diagonally upward, at the bottom of the feminine triad.... Feel you resonance of light as infinite love, and with your crystalline hands implant the substance ether throughout your circuit system....

Hold your grounding cord as you consciously journey in your lightbody across to the midway station, the star system in the lower middle portion of the triad of balance.... Feel your light in this star system, as its interstellar perception is one of the missing links to the conscious realization of all that you are, as an intergalactic lifestream.... With your crystalline hands implant the substance ether into your circuit system....

With grounding cord in hand, journey in your lightbody to the androgynous masculine sun, across to the star system at the bottom of the masculine triad.... Feel your resonant pulsation of light, as infinite love, and with your crystalline hands implant the interstellar substance ether throughout your circuit system....

Expand your awareness to encompass these 3 star systems, and energetically overlay their encodements into the central meridian of your spinal column.... Through your fingertips, seal these encodements with gold-platinum light....

In this moment be fully present with your light as it emanates the activity of creation from the androgynous feminine sun, midway station and the androgynous masculine sun, and then continue your journey to pleiades....

Hold your grounding cord as you journey in your lightbody to pleiades, a cosmic portal diagonally upward to the middle star system in the triad of balance.... Energetically feel your resonance of light within this interplanetary civilization.... With your crystalline hands implant the substance ether into your spinal column....

With grounding cord in hand, journey in your galactic lightbody to antares, diagonally upward to the middle star system in the feminine triad.... Balance the polarization between light and dark, and with your crystalline hands implant the interstellar substance ether throughout your circuit system....

Hold your grounding cord as you journey in your lightbody to arcturus, diagonally across to the middle star system in the masculine triad.... Energetically feel your resonant pulsation of light within this interplanetary civilization.... With your crystalline hands implant ether into the main power current of your spinal column, and energetically overlay the encodement of these 3 systems into your circuit system.... Through your fingertips, seal these encodements with your resonant pulsation of gold-platinum light....

Take a moment, and be fully present with your experience, as you emanate your pulsation of light throughout the star systems pleiades, antares and arcturus, then continue your journey to sirius....

✡

With grounding cord in hand, journey in your galactic lightbody to sirius, the star system above pleiades in the upper middle portion of the triad of balance.... Feel your resonant pulsation of light in this star system, as it is another missing link to the conscious knowing of all that you are, as an intergalactic lifestream.... With your crystalline hands implant the substance ether throughout your circuit system....

Hold your grounding cord as you consciously journey in your lightbody upward along the triad of balance to the next star system, the galactic core.... Intuitively sense your light within this system, as it is the ultimate missing link to the conscious realization of the true lineage of your intergalactic origin... Synergize its vertical and horizontal frequencies, and with your crystalline hands implant the interstellar substance ether into the main power current of your spinal column....

Expand your awareness to encompass these 2 star systems, and with your crystalline hands, energetically overlay their encodements into your main power current.... Through your fingertips, seal these encodements with gold-platinum light....

In this moment be fully present with your light, as you emanate it throughout the star systems sirius and galactic core, then continue your journey to alpha....

Hold your grounding cord, and consciously journey in your lightbody to alpha, the star system at the top of the feminine triad.... With grounding cord in hand, journey in your lightbody to its divine complement omega, the star system at the top of the masculine triad.... Expand your perception beyond earth life, and experience the beginning without end as the nothing and everything....

With your crystalline hands implant the substance ether, and energetically overlay the interstellar encodement from these 2 systems into your circuit system.... Through your fingertips, seal these encodements with your own resonance of gold-platinum light....

Take a moment, and be fully present with your experience of the new cycle of life, and emanate your resonance of light from the star systems alpha and omega, then continue your journey to the 13th star system, omnigalactic source....

✡

With grounding cord in hand, journey in your galactic lightbody to omnigalactic source, the star system at the top of the triad of balance.... Energetically feel your resonance of light in this star system, as the seed of creation, ain soph or.... With your crystalline hands implant the substance ether into your circuit system....

Expand your light throughout this star system, and with your crystalline hands energetically overlay the interstellar encodement of this system, into the main power current of your spinal column... Through your fingertips, seal this encodement with your own resonance of gold-platinum light.... With absolute certainty, declare the following spoken word:

> *"I AM* the light
> of omnigalactic source, and
> emanate the seed of creation, ain soph or,
> as divinity within form."

Feel your light spin your electron particles at a minimum of 3,500,000 vibrations per mono-second.... Energetically feel your resonant pulsation of gold-platinum light in the center of the vesica piscis, and command its 2 overlapping discs to spin.... Amplify your electron particle spin towards 3,800,000 vibrations per mono-second, and feel your light accelerate throughout your circuit system....

With grounding cord in hand, complete your return journey to the new earth in your galactic lightbody.... Shift your awareness to the earth-star, and replace your cord in its center.... Energetically feel your resonance of light within 13 star systems and emanate it throughout the main power current of your spinal column....

When ready, bring your awareness to where you are in the moment, and breathe into your experience of heaven on earth.... Welcome yourself home, and know you can visit any star system in the earth's galaxy whenever your heart calls you.

If you desire to further your journey in the galactic lightbody, focus your awareness on the next illustration, *Star Map*. Flow with the stream of your consciousness as it weaves in and out 5 unknown universes and their star systems.... As you experience this interstellar journey, synergize your own resonance of light within these systems.... In this moment, energetically feel synergy within your consciousness, and be fully present with your experience....

When ready, bring your awareness to wherever you are, and ground your energy in the center of the earth-star

✡   ✡   ✡

Star Map

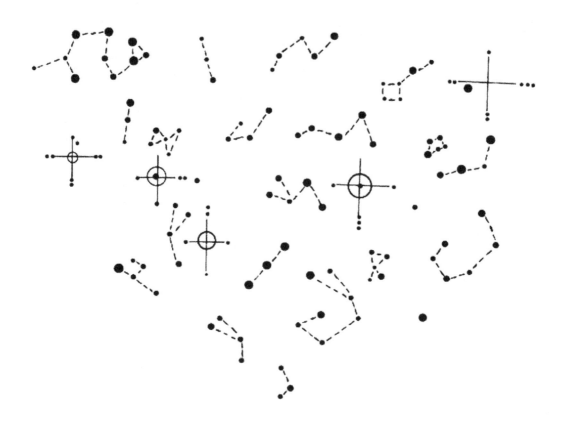

As the infinite presence ain soph or,
we live as conscious masters
in full dominion of our lives.
We experience all-that-is,
as heaven on the new earth.

Matrix of Life on the New Earth

Spherical Space: A New Configuration in the Cosmos

Everything is always in divine order; as consciousness transforms we experience major transformation in every phase of day-to-day life, as we have yet to fully understand the divine plan that we are participating in.

As dimensions fuse with one another, the collapse of space and its all-pervasive impact on our consciousness transfigures the old concept, that multiplicities within time and space are a unified continuum of no-time and no-space. The concept of spherical space transforms this perspective, as it exemplifies the cohesion of adhesive energy, and introduces another advanced concept to assist us in our understanding of the new configuration for the unified continuum; this new configuration is so fluid that it shifts us into yet, another continuum of spherical space, where time is non-existent and there is no-space at all.

Spherical space intertwines with interstellar grids of light; therefore, as we experience this new configuration we live in intergalactic timelines without confined boundaries, as well as attend to our responsibilities and commitments in day-to-day life on earth. Therefore, as we adjust to this advanced continuum of spherical space we; *expect the unexpected, as constant change is the only stable condition*. Our acceptance of this awareness is essential if we desire to catapult ourselves into the new matrix of multidimensional life.

Synchronicity of Every Moment

The key to the past is acceptance and the stargate to the future is synchronicity with all that is authentic and real. As we consciously embrace every moment, reminiscence of the past, projection of a future reality or imagining an altered reality come together as one—we experience the synchronicity of every moment rather than project thoughts, images or alternate realities that are directed by the mind.

Synchronicity in every moment reflects ultimate balance, which guides us to whatever is appropriate. This sparks further synchronicity as each moment shifts into the next without any point of reference. As we flow with our synchronistic experiences we manage our energy in every moment rather than our time.

Threshold to Our Full Potential

Possibilities and probabilities are the full creative diversity of multiple potentialities; therefore, all that we genuinely intend to create fully manifests through a fertile matrix of light.

This threshold stretches our awareness towards the use of holographic encodements; such as, clarity, focus and concentration, as each code ignites our creative fire and supports our innate ability to manifest our full potential. Are you in the midst of creating a solid foundation for your creative diversity?

Everything is energy and that which we focus attention upon takes form within matter. With every clear intention we consciously tune-in to an advanced alchemical formula that governs the quality of our creation, as it requires a resonant pulsation of light to magnetically attract similarity. Regardless of the similarity, atoms and molecules energetically respond to this unseen formula, as it transmutes their nuclei and perfects their constitution.

Fertile matrices of light convert and reconfigure components according to the needs of the moment. Each matrix sustains this advanced element, which enhances our ability to fully experience alchemy (el-ka-mi). We manifest matter (el) through the appropriate use of energy (ka) and bring its matrix of light into full consciousness (mi).

Every creation within matter alters on a quantum level and manifests through a concentrated energetic focus that commands it into existence. It is essential that we use this advanced form of energetic technology, with full integrity, so that we create what we need in the moment that it is required.

Consider this: if we sustain a perfected thoughtform without expectation, and infuse this passion into a fertile matrix of light, the mind detaches from desire and manifestation occurs in accordance with divine timing. However, only the present moment determines its outcome.

With absolute certainty, declare the following spoken word:

✿   ✿   ✿

"I AM a conscious creator.
Through clarity, focus and concentration,
pure intention manifests as form."

✿   ✿   ✿

Matrix of New Systems

The systems that govern the new matrix of life are unlike the economic or political organizations that govern 3rd dimensional reality. As we transfigure obsolete procedures into collective unity it appears as if there is a loss at the material level, however just the opposite is true. Every aspect of life flourishes with vitality and newness, and those lifestreams who implement new principles in the creation of the new matrix of life reap the reward of a spiritually rich and full life.

As we create these new principles, an all-encompassing interstellar encodement reinforces the necessity for an advanced system of order. This infusion of collective unity restructures institutions that require harmonious interactions such as: those within technology, science, spirituality, environment, government, finance, education, allopathic and holistic, kinetic theory, architecture, industry, transportation and conscious community. Each institution is responsible for providing efficient, self-sustained systems that emanate equality, balance, harmony and a sense of unity among those involved, all of which are essential to the new matrix of life.

The lifestreams responsible for the development of these new systems implement new values and principles that influence the entire global community. Because they function with integrity, honor, and reverence for all life, they demand that complete restoration take place throughout all institutions, governing nations and ethnic cultures.

These systems transfigure self-interest and ideological superiority, and create harmonious interactions of unity so that we fulfill our destiny and experience the purpose of our mission.

Advanced Encodements of Light

Advanced encodements of light necessitate harmonious action with all lifestreams; therefore, the wars of ignorance between different races, cultures and religious sects are non-existent.

These encodements directly influence us through the physical attributes of: joy, freedom, spontaneity, creativity, passion, integrity, honor, equality, spiritual fulfillment, divine will, synchronicity, synergy, conscious mastery, divinity and infinite love. The more we abide by these codes, the more we emanate divine grace to all those with whom we come in contact. Are you ready to emanate infinite love towards others?

To those lifestreams whose purpose it is to facilitate awareness of these new encodements and implement them into society, we are in deep gratitude.

Advanced Technology

Technology on the new earth exponentially expands throughout the 21st century, and continuous development of the microchip, supercomputers, and solar and wind technology facilitates this forward momentum of progress. This era of advanced technological evolution initiates the manifestation of off-planet technology in all systems on the new earth.

As this advanced technology solidifies, it emanates through the consciousness of those lifestreams whose intergalactic mission it is to implement advanced knowledge into a newly formed society.

To all of you, we are eternally grateful.

Science

In the new matrix of life all areas of science transfigure to include the dynamics that reign on the new earth. Mathematicians apply complex encodements into their work and integrate this knowledge into many of the new systems. Geometricians facilitate us in our study and use of geometric designs. Physicists study altered laws of physics, and chemists revise their base of knowledge through the study of cosmic substances. Geneticists decode the configuration of light in the original 12-strand dna. Biologists use their abilities to map and record procreation for the new human species, as well as the fauna and flora that is present on the new earth. Geologists are fully aware of the new forms of advanced interstellar technologies as they monitor new waves of resonant pulsations in the magnetic and electromagnetic grids, ley lines, vortices and the tectonic plates. Meteorologists attune to the thrust of atmospheric activities and accurately alert us to impending natural occurrences. Astrophysicists apply interstellar technology to their understanding of space travel and modify it for widespread use in our civilization, while cosmologists facilitate the assimilation of intergalactic communion with lifestreams in other star systems, galaxies and universes.

To those lifestreams in the field of science who initiate multiple dynamics to shift us into the 21st century, we are in deep gratitude.

Spirituality

In the new matrix of life spiritual teachings from traditional paradigms and religious doctrines transfigure into a unified concept of holiness. Under the guidance of oversoul, we interact as one consciousness, function in harmonious action with one another, and emanate infinite love through the attributes of equality and freedom.

New awareness of our expanded sense of spirituality enables us to support each other in the remembrance of on- and off-planet experiences; therefore, as a unified team of conscious lifestreams we uphold the light while we fulfill our purpose.

We give credence to our destiny and declare our liberation, which encourages us to be forthright in our independent thinking. As conscious lifestreams we tread farther into the unknown in support of the divine plan.

To all of you who work so diligently to sustain your light on earth, we are eternally grateful.

Environment

The new earth's environment is free of all chemical substance and imbalance from disturbances of environmental chaos. This restoration transfigures the oxygen in the air into an air-based frequency of light. The frequency within this light comprises the interstellar substance, icosa-dodecahedron, which naturally cleanses earth's waters, soil and air, and restores these elements into their original perfection.

To those lifestreams whose purpose it is to activate change in our environment and fully develop innovative systems that reform earth's ecosystem, we are in deep gratitude.

Government

In the new matrix of life the new system of government emanates the multidimensional principle, as above, is below. Therefore, we elect a spiritual government that unites our civilization. These politicians serve their constituents with a true sense of spiritual purpose, and govern for the highest good of the new earth and its inhabitants. They support the desires of the whole and through their integrity make certain that political power remains in the hands of the people. As we create this new system of government, we see the profound impact that it has on our interplanetary civilization.

To all of you who effortlessly work to implement a spiritual government that administers the decisions made solely by the people, for the people, we are eternally grateful.

Financial System

Transfiguration of earth's financial system is a global endeavor, which results in an equal distribution of wealth. As we develop refined financial institutions that eliminate greed at every level, we facilitate the development of a highly advanced universal monetary system that emanates integrity and financially supports all lifestreams equally.

To those lifestreams whose purpose it is to initiate this new monetary formula, which equally distributes its wealth among all people, we are in deep gratitude.

Allopathic and Holistic Systems

The new system for the medical profession advances toward the use of highly developed technology to maintain the influx of patients requiring this service.

Many medical professionals have yet to realize that we are releasing energetic patterns that are dormant within our cells, in full preparation for our experiences in the new matrix of life. However, disease may be relevant in many lifestreams, therefore, any medical diagnosis that is physiologically-based or life-threatening, may require the patient to receive allopathic treatment. It is the patients right to decide the way in which they prefer to approach their own method of healing. Some medical diseases are chronic or self-created, and in the world of holistic health and wellness, this reveals that the issue may be energetically based rather than a medical problem.

In the chinese medical system professionals receive monetary compensation when their patients are well, rather than when they are sick. As medical professionals within the western system refine their approach to wellness and eliminate their policies based in financial greed, they genuinely integrate the use of advanced energetic technologies, which support complete collaboration between allopathic and holistic practices.

Professionals involved in either practice approach their work with heart-based sensitivity, and tune into the required solution that facilitates a deeper level of healing for the patient, rather than prescribe advice purely from book knowledge.

Certain holistic institutions manufacture advanced bio-magnetic products, such as those that counteract low-level radiation from electromagnetic fields. These products contain high frequencies or resonant pulsations of light that facilitate change in our electromagnetic and magnetic energy fields. Some of these vibrational products are taken internally and others are energetic tools that protect our electromagnetic energy from toxic forms of radiation.

In the new matrix of life those lifestreams who participate in the holistic profession are in service to the highest good of all and do so with infinite love. Their humanitarian mission is to integrate the use of light as an advanced form of energetic technology into appropriate methodologies that use high-tech equipment, so that both allopathic and holistic systems effectively serve the welfare of all. The new encodement for health and well-being is to accept full responsibility for ourselves, and maintain a healthy life force that reinforces wellness beyond our present awareness.

To all of you who effortlessly apply your diligence to initiate a unified system of allopathic and holistic methodologies that enable lifestreams to take charge of their own health and well-being, we are eternally grateful.

Education System

The new education system transfigures generally accepted knowledge and information so that we assimilate the advanced technology required for the new matrix of life. It offers the appropriate energetic curriculums and training so that we remember our original innate abilities from lifetimes in other interplanetary civilizations. This implies that we must amplify our resonant pulsation of light to its highest available frequency.

The frequency of this new system manifests on the new earth through some of the crystal children that incarnate as golden age teachers. They have the innate ability to initiate this new system and deliver its cosmic intelligence to those who are open to accept the concept. Until we remember our intergalactic abilities and train ourselves to participate in multidimensional experiences on the new earth, it is imperative that we accept the guided direction of these gifted children. Are you willing to be taught the essential curriculum by an advanced soul who may be in the body of a child?

Crystal children bring to earth a new curriculum within this system that includes the remembrance of how to implement advanced forms of interstellar technologies from experiences in other interplanetary civilizations. Through our resonant pulsation of light we remember how to neutralize off-planet stellar patterns that influence our well-being.

New encodements in the educational system also enable us to receive training in the advanced use of kinesis. Lifestreams guide themselves to the kinetics that resonates, and golden age teachers support them as they activate their knowing of how to use a specific technique within the art of kinesis. This advanced training along with other curriculum is available to all regardless of age, race or creed.

Through this new education system, we are energetically guided by the most profound training of all—our own. Through our inner knowing we manifest advanced forms of interstellar technology that are new to earth; therefore it is essential that we welcome our new gifts with wonder and enthusiasm.

To those lifestreams whose purpose it is to initiate curriculums that enable us to remember our intergalactic training and use this knowing to assist others in society, we are in deep gratitude.

Kinesis

The genetic structure within our original configuration of dna transfigures ancient techniques and modalities into advanced energetic technologies. As the gap between thought and manifestation lessens, advanced forms of kinetics intertwine with one another, and are prominent to our new way of life.

The principle of kinesis transfigures energy, which used appropriately, transcends matter. Its alchemical configuration derives from a resonant pulsation of light that alters matter on a quantum level. If we modify, add to or completely rebuild a base underlying energy formation, it instantly manifests a corresponding resonant pulsation of light. As our light infuses with some of this kinetics we vary in accordance with the way we synergize the appropriate pulsation.

Through focus and concentration, we bring forth our innate ability to use these advanced forms of kinetic technology. Some of these techniques are within us waiting to be awakened, and others manifest within our awareness from other timelines of experience. These technologies are advanced in nature and the ability to use them manifests through the lifestreams that contract to bring them into fruition on the new earth.

Following is a general overview of the structure of kinesis:

Aerokinesis—purify air and direct the course of wind and gasses;

Aquakinesis—generate movement in water;

Atmokinesis—influence atmosphere and weather;

Audiokinesis—transfigure sound waves;

Bi-locate—experience of being in more than one location simultaneously; multidimensional version of astral projection;

Biokinesis—transfigure organs and other biological matter; skilled biokinetics alter genetic encodement, which transfigures the appearance and functionality of the body;

Cryokinesis—manifest freezing temperatures and control cold air; when cryokinetics apply this ability to water, they form ice;

Echokinesis—measurement of acoustic pulsations in air and water to determine distances; echokinetics use sonar feedback to visualize and create spatial mapping;

Electrokinesis—generate and control electrical currents through the use of the mind; electrokinetics recharge or transfigure electricity from electronically-based devices;

Geokinesis—alteration of mineral composition; natural geokinetics are alchemists that release energy between tectonic plates;

Gyrokinesis—realignment of gravitational fields of energy;

Hydrokinesis—alter liquids such as water, oil and alcohol; hydrokinetics increase or decrease the momentum of water;

Levitation—state of awareness through which we defy gravity and suspend our physical bodies in the air; levitation is a form of telekinesis;

Magnetism—energetically channels the flow of resonant frequencies throughout the physical body;

Magnokinesis—create and transfigure electromagnetic grids;

Photokinesis—create and alter light; become invisible at will; change colors by transmutation of light; skilled photokinetics shift the light spectrum within the unified circuit system;

Psychokinesis—alter energy, matter, vibration and recorded time; psychokinetics sustain the full range of kinetic ability to greater or lesser degrees;

Pyrokinesis—control of extreme hot temperatures; skilled pyrokinetics use varying resonant pulsations of light that create temperature increases in all forms of matter; create and direct fire at will;

Remote viewing—projection from a single physical location that views a 3D event, as it occurs within the unified continuum;

Telekinesis—alter gravity and electromagnetic fields; skilled telekinetics move physical objects within their present location as well as at a distance;

Telepathy—energetic exchange of our resonant frequencies of cosmic intelligence in this and other interplanetary civilizations;

Teleportation—ability to instantaneously travel from one location to another; assimilation of magnetic and electromagnetic frequencies of light; form dematerializes and rematerializes at will, as it travels to and from other interplanetary civilizations;

Thermokinesis—generate warmth and heat; skilled thermokinetics alter objective or subjective temperature;

Vitakinesis—alter life force within the kingdom of nature;

Beyond Kinesis—to those lifestreams whose purpose it is to initiate the above resonant pulsations of advanced kinesis, we are in deep gratitude for your service. To those lifestreams whose destiny it is to bring forth interstellar technologies, which are far beyond the known modalities of kinesis, we hold sincere gratitude to you for sustaining the pulsations of light that are absolutely essential for these downloads.

Architecture

In the new matrix of life architectural design is very diverse and comprises technology that is suitable for life in the 21st century. As we implement the use of this technology we download designs into our awareness to assist us in the development of new cities. These cities comprise corporate buildings, schools, home environments and architectural structures that are primarily of round, domed marble buildings, embedded with sacred designs leafed in gold.

These structures are designed by architects who transmit and receive specific matrices of light that manifest off-planet structure into form. These matrices sustain relatively intricate patterns with walls leafed in gold and windows that reflect the full spectrum of light. Inside some of these finished structures there are sacred healing temples that emanate lemurian codes through crystal pillars, obelisks and spheres. These temples sustain exceptionally high frequencies with resonant pulsations of light that magnetically attract those lifestreams who desire to live and work with this technology.

The systems within these structures operate through highly-developed computer technology, with amplified frequencies that operate through voice control or the touch of a button.

To all of you who build the essential structures and homes required for life in the 21st century and provide the technology to maintain them, we are eternally grateful.

Industry

All industry operates through a model of full integrity and refined service, and complies with the standards that are essential for a healthy environment.

In the new matrix of life the use of high-tech equipment programmed with advanced technology creates highly efficient industries, and facilitates all operating systems such as commercial production, manufacturing, inventory and deliveries.

Lifestreams employed in the area of industrial corporation inform their market of available products and services through the use of advanced technology and its electronic broadcasting. As a result, we follow our inner guidance as we determine what our requirements are and complete our purchases accordingly.

To those lifestreams whose purpose it is to initiate and maintain high levels of integrity and refined service within corporations on the new earth, we are in deep gratitude.

Transportation

Inventors, astrophysicists and engineers use their skills collectively to fulfill a purpose greater than they achieve on their own. As an effective unit these professionals bring their knowledge together, master magnetics and build vehicles that function electrically or as hybrid. As a result of their creativity transportation is greatly enhanced.

In the new matrix of life this system of movement is powered by advanced technology, as well as through thought. Knowledge and use of interstellar technologies facilitate in the development of spacecrafts, which enables us to travel between interplanetary civilizations. These new methods are essential to our existence as they assist in a more rapid method of travel from one destination to another, as well as in innate ability to teleport from one star system to another. Does the advanced concept of this method of excursion excite you?

To all of you who master the magnetics to build vehicles and essential spacecrafts that operate through the use of interstellar technology, as well as initiate space travel that takes lifestreams into other star systems, galaxies and universes—we are in deep gratitude.

Conscious Community

In the new matrix of life we create a new society based on balanced living in communities that strengthen the concept of equality, regardless of another's ethnic background or creed.

Conscious communities create morals that comprise a unified level of integrity, and as employers and employees we interact in ways that support equality for all. Each community maintains independent living for all involved, and encourages the sharing of wisdom and knowledge, as well as ideas and talents between the multitudes of professionals who live there. As professionals we combine our expertise with genuine authenticity and are in service to the greater good of all. We strengthen our connection with self-sufficient, ecologically-minded and like-minded lifestreams within the community; such as, politicians, lawyers, doctors, pharmacists, engineers, writers, artists, plumbers, carpenters, mechanics, gardeners, nurses, massage therapists, healers, counselors, teachers, coaches, chefs, waitresses and so on. As a result of this sense of unity, we emanate infinite love towards thy neighbor.

We observe life from a global perspective and offer our support as we make a difference on the new earth. We develop global centers that form circles of unity based in common ground. These centers emanate infinite love for the needs of the whole and provide a greater sense of financial stability, health and well-being to all who participate.

To those lifestreams whose purpose it is to establish these communities and maintain high levels of integrity and service on the new earth, we are in deep gratitude.

New Encodement for Intimate Relationships

In the new matrix of life we synergize the frequency of another encodement that compliments the perfection of intimate relationships on the new earth. *All* relationships integrate this encodement so that we energetically feel the resonant pulsation of the twin-ray through which the fire of creation births one spark of light. *Through our unique cosmic dance we come full circle and energetically blend the pulsation of the twin-ray within ourselves.*

This resonant pulsation of light has a profound personal impact on our lives, and as we synchronize with its frequency we activate an unfamiliar threshold that fully supports the next level of our true intimacy. This profound activation impacts our grid system and facilitates an in-depth understanding of the distinctions between soulmates, the purpose of twin-flames and the new encodement for our intimate relationship with the beloved complement.

As we synchronize with this resonant pulsation of our light, we naturally interact through the language of light that emanates from the heart. This sensitive human organ is the unified compass that synchronizes our physiological and cerebral-emotional circuitry. It supports the experience of initiation and completion and keeps us mindful that this is the ultimate purpose for the beloved complement relationship.

If we truly desire to synchronize with our resonant pulsation of light in the twin-ray, it is essential that we synergize the encodement that enables us to manifest a cherished relationship with the beloved complement.

Intimate Relationship with the Beloved Complement

The new matrix of life supports the blissful union with the ultimate of all intimate relationships—the beloved complement. *In order to manifest this perfect partner in our life we must first be the perfect partner.*

As the perfect partner we are free of all encumbrances that hinder the perfection of enlightenment within ourselves, which means we are whole and complete within ourselves.

Most of humanity searches for this ultimate partnership—an intimate, romantic, symbiotic connection that nurtures our soul through the joyous attributes of balance, harmony, equality and synchronicity. While all beloved complements experience this energetic connection, each relationship sustains its own dynamic.

Our resonance of light as beloved complements births through the twin-ray. *One of the beloved complements emanates initiation and the other radiates completion;* this enables both partners to magnetically attract one another in accordance with divine timing. This captivating attraction transfigures 2 individual circuit systems into one unified configuration of light; therefore, both partners share an indivisible system of circuitry, yet sustain their individual pulsation of light. One partner transmits interstellar balance, while the other, consciously or unconsciously, unifies their circuit system in the physical world.

Before beloved complements manifest their relationship in the physical, their individual frequencies weave in and out, from side-to-side, or flow forward and backward within this etheric loop. Ultimately both frequencies merge in the center of this configuration, and in this divine moment the relationship anchors its light so that it physically manifests into present reality.

Comprehension of this completed circuitry is better understood by energetically feeling your resonant pulsation of light through the use of the key, *Emanate Your Light Throughout Infinity,* which follows this section.

The concept of a completed circuit system between intimate partners is a rare experience for lifestreams on earth, yet the manifestation of this relationship is essential to those lifestreams who live on the new earth. This unified circuit system requires that each complement ultimately understands and accepts, through conscious preference to be with one another, that the energetic frequency flowing between them completes their circuitry, as one.

As complements approach the divine timing of their physical connection, there is a magnetic pull that facilitates an energetic amplification within their frequencies. This brings forth the conscious awareness that the physical manifestation of this ultimate relationship is imminent. This prompts the valid question: What does this cherished relationship look and feel like?

The beloved complement relationship is the capstone of intimacy, and as equals, we share a profound love for one another. This ultimate resonance of love pulsates throughout our cells as they dance in pure joy, regardless of physical distance. As we energetically feel this finely tuned quality of intimacy, we drink the alchemical elixir that comes from the richness and fullness of a shared cup, yet our life together is independent of the other. We enhance and enrich one another, and bring meaning and purpose to our relationship rather than expecting something from it. As we weave our lives together we form a duet where one partner plays melody and the other partner brings in harmony. Our hearts blend together, as one heart and our sexual intimacy sustains a sacred focus that emanates a magnificent rose-colored light throughout infinity.

The beloved complement relationship is more than the coming together of 2 lifestreams; it enhances a profound and highly advanced soul-to-soul connection that emanates beyond words. Are you ready to manifest this quality of intimacy in your life?

Key: Emanate Your Light Throughout Infinity

In this key you energetically feel your resonant pulsation of light in the center of a sacred symbol, the figure 8 on its side.

✿　✿　✿

Envision a configuration of light in the shape of a figure 8 on its side.... Shift your awareness to one of the loops in this configuration, and energetically feel your own resonant pulsation of light within it....

While your consciousness is on one of the loops, envision an illumined path of white light and walk in the light towards the other loop.... While on the loop, continue to walk towards the center of this configuration, where you energetically feel your resonant pulsation of white light....

With your consciousness in the center of this white light, energetically feel your own resonance of light emanate from this neutral point, and radiate it to your beloved complement.... Feel your light penetrate their circuit system, and then let the sensation go.... Take a moment, and be fully present with your experience....

Through conscious intention and with absolute certainty, declare the following spoken word:

> *"I AM* the one that emanates initiation, and
> *I AM* the one that radiates completion.
> As the capstone of intimacy
> we are one configuration of light."

Feel your light spin your electron particles at a minimum of 3,800,000 vibrations.... Energetically feel your resonant pulsation of gold-platinum light in the center of the vesica piscis, and command its 2 overlapping discs to spin.... Amplify your electron particle spin towards 4,000,000 vibrations, and feel your light emanate throughout infinity....

Shift your awareness to the center of the earth-star, and feel your light within it.... Energetically feel your resonant pulsation of light within earth's magnetic energy, and ground it into your physiological circuitry....

When ready, bring your awareness to where you are in the moment, and breathe into your experience.

✿ ✿ ✿

Interstellar Configuration for Infinity

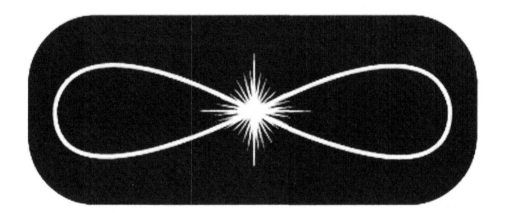

Communion of Our Intergalactic Origin

The new matrix of life enables us to live that which is foretold among the stars, and directs us to further frontiers, where the unknown becomes known. As we remember what star system, galaxy or universe we come from, we receive the most precious gift of all, awareness of the true lineage of our intergalactic origin.

Throughout the 21st century the landings of numerous spacecrafts previously cloaked in earth's sky are regular occurrences. Although this perception is a phenomenal stretch for most of us to comprehend, the new matrix of life requires that we remain centered and balanced as we experience actual visitations. These visitations are a natural part of multidimensional life, and they support the solid foundation required for intergalactic communication on the new earth. Our full acceptance of these visitations reveals the understanding that as intergalactic lifestreams, we are emissaries from civilizations beyond this galaxy and travel many light years to welcome ourselves home. And, we remember that we are a race of interplanetary citizens that honors and respects the true lineage of our intergalactic origin.

As we jointly participate in this long-awaited cosmic celebration and homecoming, we finally stand side-by-side in cosmic synergy with intergalactic family. Our resonant pulsation of light fully supports us, and we energetically feel an already established synchronicity in the intergalactic realm. Our innate ability to project laser beams of light through the cosmic eye, transmit communication through thought, and energetically feel resonant pulsations of light from other solar systems, is a natural way of life.

With absolute certainty, declare the following spoken word:

✿   ✿   ✿

"*I AM* galactic self,
in human embodiment."

✿   ✿   ✿

Personal Galactic Symbol

Consciously or unconsciously, our personal galactic symbol gradually weaves in and out of our awareness. Its manifestation occurs through cosmic dispensation, so forget the human desire to create the symbol that you think you need, and be open to energetically synergize the dispensation of the symbol that is appropriate for you.

Our personal galactic symbol is sacred to our interstellar connection, and as it naturally becomes visible through our inner sight it downloads and regulates the assimilation of interstellar light. It is essential that we use this symbol to align our circuit system, as well as neutralize the energy of the items that we bring into our environment and personal living space. In doing so, we further amplify our own resonant pulsation of light so that it assimilates interstellar encodements.

Once you fully assimilate the frequency of your galactic symbol, inner guidance directs you to its appropriate use in every moment. Are you ready to have this symbol in your day-to-day life?

Life as a Conscious Master

Life as a conscious master requires that we expand our awareness from being the center of our universe to encompass the full scope of life on the new earth.

If you feel as though you have been on an intense journey of spiritual evolution, well, you are right. It takes eons of lifetimes to attain conscious mastery, and now that you remember the true lineage of your intergalactic origin, you are fully present on the new earth for the most miraculous experience of all; our new way of life holds an exciting adventure for all of us, so hang on to your hat.

As conscious masters we maintain a neutral point of interstellar balance. For the 1st time throughout the evolution of humanity, soul fully descends into the physical body, while in embodiment, and we are conscious enough to experience both realms of awareness simultaneously. This often feels as if we are permanently earthbound yet, the truth is, as the sovereign breath of creation, we are fully present as consciousness on the new earth.

We view life through the eyes of unity, engage in the jubilance of cosmic interplay and energetically feel the cosmic cadence in balance and synchronicity with day-to-day life. We are aware of the true purpose of life and have insight into the knowing that everything manifests in accordance with divine timing. We:

✡   ✡   ✡

Accept our rightful position in the hall of masters.

Live in accordance with divine will.

Realize that our mind attaches to nothing, yet is surprised by everything.

Impart an unfolding concept that views life through the eyes of oneness.

Emanate infinite love with full conscious knowing.

Respect others and their right to choose their experiences.

Remain in service to the greater good of all.

Support others in their adjustment to the new matrix of life.

Understand our purpose in the grand scope of life.

Act with integrity, truth, honor and commitment.

Know that everything is always in divine order.

Expect the unexpected as constant change is the only stable condition.

✡   ✡   ✡

Are you ready to do what you love as well as love what you do with every fiber of your being?

Through the following chart, observe 5 universal equations with counterparts that comprise vital attributes for life as a conscious master on the new earth.

Divinity				_Sovereignty_
Freedom	+	change	=	synchronicity
Acceptance	+	truth	=	authenticity
Balance	+	clarity	=	cosmic intelligence
Oneness	+	knowing	=	synergy
Mastery	+	divinity	=	sovereignty

Key: Emanate Mastery

In this key you consciously emanate your own mastery.

✿   ✿   ✿

Energetically feel your resonant pulsation of light, as infinite love….

Envision a crystal clear diamond in the center of your heart…. Focus your awareness in the center of this diamond, and feel the attributes of freedom and change, acceptance and truth, balance and clarity, oneness and knowing, and mastery

239

and divinity, then emanate their pulsation throughout infinity....

While your consciousness is still in the center of this diamond, energetically feel your resonant pulsations of light, as ain soph or, and as this sovereign breath of creation, declare the following spoken word:

> *"I AM* a conscious master, and
> live life through the attributes of
> innocence, humility, simplicity,
> joy and passion.
> Graduation day is at hand.
> All that *I AM*
> emanates as the sovereign breath of creation,
> ain soph or.
> *I AM* home."

Energetically feel your resonant pulsation of gold-platinum light in the center of the vesica piscis, and command its 2 overlapping discs to spin.... Amplify your electron particle spin beyond 4,000,000 vibrations per mono-second, and accelerate your light throughout infinity.... Consciously feel your own resonance of infinity, and bring yourself home so that you enlighten the new earth.... Take a deep breath, and be fully present with your experience....

Shift your awareness to the center of the earth-star, and with humility, ground your light into the earth-star....

When ready, bring your awareness to where you are in the moment.... Be consciously aware of your sense of wholeness, and fully emanate your mastery of heaven on the new earth.

✡   ✡   ✡

In Conclusion, Yet an Endless Journey

"As we continue to cross further thresholds
from the known into the unknown,
we remember our consciousness within other universes."

The new matrix of life requires that we stretch our awareness and perceive all that we are beyond this universe. As we synergize the notion of this advanced perspective, our consciousness emanates from the center of this universe and encompasses life in other universes. As interplanetary citizens on the new earth, our new prototype entices us with the rightful passage to explore life in star systems within star systems, galaxies within galaxies and universes within universes.

The grand finale of life as we know it is complete, and as for how we fully participate in the matrix of multidimensional awareness, we as a new species, are going to find out. What some of us already know is that the application of instinctive data, with reference to our remembrance of intergalactic consciousness, further refines that we experience life as a continuous passageway.

All that *I AM* knows that the grand scope of life shifts us beyond where we are in any given moment. And, as we continue to evolve into further unknowns, our resonance of light is always there to greet us when we arrive, from yet, another endless journey of experience.

Congratulations to you for your devotion and commitment to energetically feel your own pulsation of cosmic cadence. It is an honor to support you as you synergize all that you are as unified consciousness and complete your quantum shift into the new matrix of life.

From one intergalactic citizen to another, welcome home.

Many blessings,

salantra

Golden Age Glossary

activation: energetic awakening of intergalactic consciousness;

adam kadmon/adam kadmon elohim: perfection of heavenly human in physical form;

adonai elohim adonai: extension of creation manifest as singular emanation;

aerokinesis: purifies air and directs the course of wind and gasses;

age of light: matrix for the 2000 year cycle of the 7th golden age;

ain: void before creation;

ain soph: infinite space; endless boundless presence; ain means nothing before creation and soph is the final stage of manifestation;

ain soph or: infinite light; body of creation;

akashic records: etheric archive; multidimensional experiences of holographic data stored in an etheric hall of records;

alchemical elixir: spiritual nectar; resonant pulsation of light; transmits the essence of infinite love;

alchemy: alteration of physical matter through intention;

alignment: energetic orientation where the centers of what is being aligned is in balance; alignment of templates within grid systems; integration of physical, emotional, cerebral and spiritual;

alternate reality: experience within another timeline of consciousness;

androgynous: unified masculine and feminine principles of ain soph or;

androgynous principle: covenant of light between the masculine and feminine within ain soph or;

andromeda galaxy: emanates balance between vertical and horizontal frequencies of light; transmits through thought, color and sound; sensation of timelessness;

angelic emissaries of light: our resonant pulsation of light as archangels;

anunnaki: intergalactic civilization on the planet nibiru;

aquakinesis: generate movement in water;

archangels: resonant frequency of light within the tree of life; energetic bridge to the lineage of our intergalactic origin;

> **auriel:** an angelic emissary of our light that emanates cosmic order and synergy throughout consciousness;

> **gabriel:** as this consciousness we experience cosmic wisdom, circles of unity, love and service;

khamael: as this emissary of light we emanate cosmic intelligence throughout consciousness;

metatron: as this angelic emissary of light, we emanate conscious divinity in its purest form; interstellar garment of el shaddai;

mikael: as this consciousness we experience our galactic coronation and divine birthright; union, as in the crown of immortality;

raphael: our consciousness, as this emissary of light emanates true sovereignty;

ratziel: as this angelic emissary of light we experience evolution as it is within the divine plan;

sandalphon: as this consciousness we synergize earth's new blueprint into our circuit system; we embody the frequencies of all 10 sefirahs and consciously experience heaven on earth;

tzadkiel: our consciousness as this emissary of light transfigures energetic distortion into perfection;

tzaphkiel: as this angelic emissary of light, we emanate cosmic pulsations throughout the subtle circuit system;

ascension: upward mobility along a vertical axis; assimilation of original configurations of energy that realign our frequency with its original blueprint; transfigures matter and energy; brings all that we experience into the present moment; final phase of life on earth as we know it; supports our divine birthright; integrates divinity and conscious mastery; occurs in daily life experiences;

ashtar command: as the resonant frequency of the ashtar command, we are a fleet of space commanders that oversee and govern all activities between inter-planetary civilizations in this and other regions of distant universes;

astral template: subtle circuitry of complex archetypal forces, which manifest as awareness within 3rd dimensional reality; transforming crucible through which all energy passes; complex emotional circuitry that emanates resonant frequencies of light throughout the physical body;

atmic template: subtle circuitry that emanates as undifferentiated awareness within divinity; modulates amplification of christ-light throughout the circuit system; sustains a unified frequency of light;

atmokinesis: influence atmosphere and weather;

attachment: limiting force of self-imposed energetic patterns that stagnates spiritual understanding and maturity;

attunement: energetic alignment that transmutes dissonance into balance and harmony;

audiokinesis: transfigure sound waves;

belief: self-created or adopted thoughtform that strengthens our awareness or reinforces illusion;

beloved complement: resonant pulsation within the twin-ray; ultimate counterpart; intimate, romantic, symbiotic relationship that nurtures our soul through the joyous experience of balance, harmony and equality; bi-locate: experience of being in more than one location simultaneously; multidimensional version of astral projection;

biokinesis: transfigure organs and other biological matter within all life forms; skilled biokinetics alter genetic encodement, which transfigures the appearance and functionality of the body;

binah: sefirah at the top of the feminine triad;

binah ruach devekut: sacred tongue; a unified frequency; synthesis of spirit; transmutes the old paradigm into an another age of light;

blueprint: geometric grid of light that sustains interstellar encodements, as in 12-configurations of original dna; interstellar patterns of light; formless, yet all form; sustain templates from which matrices are created;

blueprint of divinity: sustains the divine plan for sovereignty;

body of creation: entirety of creation; ain soph or;

body of light: interstellar frequency of the galactic lightbody;

bridging: crossing thresholds of consciousness so that ego merges with soul;

causal template: subtle circuitry; frequency that assimilates higher self, as our light;

cellular memory: cell's innate ability to remember previous experiences;

chakratic circuitry: energetic gateways within the unified circuit system; circuitry of 7 primary gateways, 21 secondary gateways, 5 additional gateways of advanced frequencies of light; solar circuitry; subtle circuitry;

cherubim: as cherubim, we are recording angels in service to the seraphim and translate thoughtforms that emanate directly from our resonance of angelic light;

chesed: middle sefirah of the masculine triad;

chochmah: top sefirah of the masculine triad;

chohans: our consciousness within the 4th, 5th, 6th and 7th rays; as this consciousness we facilitate our evolution from the phase of the initiate to conscious mastery;

christ-light: resonance of light within the spleen; emanates infinite love and divine wisdom;

christed-oversoul template: sustains christ-light in its purest form; assimilates the language of light throughout the circuit system; energetic mediator between human consciousness and all-that-is;

circadian rhythms: behavioral and physiological rhythms associated with the cycle of the new earth's rotation;

circuit system: energetic grid system that includes physiological, chakratic and subtle circuitry;

clairaudience: hearing thoughts, words, sounds and resonant tones beyond physical auditory range from our own resonance of light in other dimensions;

clairsentience: energetic vibrations beyond the range of all physical senses; energetic sensation of resonant pulsations of light;

clairvoyance: visual insight into the range of multidimensional frequencies of light;

communion: synergy of consciousness; resonant pulsation of light within self;

complement: resonant pulsation of light in the twin-ray;

completed circuit system: completed resonant pulsation of light;

configuration of energy: original 12-strand configuration of dna; frequency or relative position of a group of planets or stars; complex matrix of light;

conscious: cognizant; active cerebral capacity; being aware of one's full presence;

conscious creation: alchemy of manifestation through intention;

conscious knowing: immediate recognition of energetic transmissions that originate beyond human intellect;

consciousness: umbrella for a multitude of frequencies; awareness of one's infinite existence;

continuum: continuous experience of an event; time-space continuum; continuum of time experienced in another dimension; past and future in the present moment;

core imprint: originates as our 1st embodied experience with soul-spark and sets into motion the stream of consciousness that accompanies soul; sustains thought-forms that create cerebral imbalance;

cosmic cross: equal cross of light that emanates interstellar pulsations of light;

cosmic eye: solar gateway in the center of the forehead;

cosmic stream: consciousness as it flows in and out of inclusion;

creative fire: flame within the fountain of creativity;

credence: declaration of inner liberation;

cryokinesis: manifest freezing temperatures and control cold air; cryokinetics change water to form ice;

crystal bridge: an energetic bridge to the new matrix of life;

crystal children: future inhabitants of the new earth; golden age teachers;

crystalline: perfected state;

dark night of soul: reconciliation of on- and off-planet remembrance; experience of phoenix rising from its ashes;

descension: soul is fully present in the physical body; resonant pulsations of unified consciousness experienced while living in 3rd dimension;

dimension: magnitude measured in a particular direction, which determines the "location of an object or event in time and space;" range of vibrational frequencies in which everything exists simultaneously; interdimensional timeline of consciousness; 1-dimensional space is a single line, 2-dimensional space is flat, 3-dimensional space has length, width and height, and 4-dimensional space synergizes space and time;

> **1st dimension:** mineral world; holds ancient knowledge within atoms, molecules, minerals and rocks; slowest vibratory rate on earth;

2nd dimension: vibrational timeline in which the stellar frequency of plants, trees, animals (on land and sea), and insects seed the earth with a grid of intelligence that is equal with human intelligence;

3rd dimension: timeline where souls incarnate into individuation to experience full conscious knowing with all-that-is; density of earth school experience; world of illusion and separation from the whole;

4th dimension: the polarized realm of archetypal forces that interact with our consciousness on earth; promotes unity and peace; guided by our consciousness in the intergalactic civilization of anunnaki on planet nibiru;

5th dimension: interstellar blueprint of light; sustains interplanetary wavelengths that surround earth, yet are invisible to the naked eye; frequencies of geometric encodement; new matrix of life; guided by our consciousness in the intergalactic civilizations of the star system pleiades;

6th dimension: sustains frequencies of sacred geometry that transmit through the language of light; is the lightbody form of the 3rd dimensional world; guided by our consciousness in the intergalactic civilizations of the star system sirius;

7th dimension: sustains light that emanates balance between vertical and horizontal energies; transmits communication through thought; stargate to intergalactic consciousness; guided by our consciousness in the intergalactic civilizations of the andromeda galaxy;

8th dimension: structural organization of cosmic intelligence, known as the intergalactic federation; dimension through which group souls fulfill their cosmic mission; guided by our consciousness in the intergalactic civilizations of the constellation orion;

9th dimension: intertwines with the most subtle of frequencies and synergizes them within the main power current of our spinal column; sustains our consciousness within the galactic core; transmits the language of light into the 3rd dimension; guided by our consciousness in the intergalactic civilization known as enochians;

10th dimension: the nothing and the everything where the 1 and the 0 are unified; emanates the alchemical formula for conscious divinity; sustains the androgynous principle that the sum is greater than its parts;

11th dimension: synergy of 2 distinct frequencies, the androgynous masculine principle of yhvh and the androgynous feminine principle of shekinah, as the unified frequency of yhsvh;

12th dimension: an endless perspective; emanates the resonant frequency of 12 configurations of energy; synergizes all 12 dimensions into the 13th dimension;

13th dimension: everything is equal to the whole; all time, all space, all consciousness, all knowing, all experience exist as one; an inevitable state of awareness that brings us full circle;

dissonance: inharmonious energy; discord;

divine: spiritual aspect of all-that-is; inner presence of light; supreme being;

divine order: universal order; order in which all things naturally occur;

divine plan: implementation of cosmic order;

divine will: transfiguration of free will; conscious alignment with the divine plan; overrides distortion created by the egoic-mind; in alignment with the highest good of all; fusion of soul contract and destiny pattern;

dna: the master molecule that contains the original genetic blueprint of divinity; deoxyribonucleic acid;

dodecahedron: platonic solid with 12 faces to its design; sustains the frequency for the interstellar substance ether;

duality: state of polarization that reinforces co-dependence and creates opposite polarities;

earth-star: an energetic gateway 6 - 12 inches below the arches of the feet;

echokinesis: measurement of acoustic pulsations in air and water to determine distances; use of sonar feedback to visualize and create spatial mapping;

ego: attachment to who we are as form; false identification; controls thoughts and behavior of self-importance; perpetuates the illusion of separation; focuses on duality and polarity consciousness; projects an unclear perception;

egoic template: subtle circuitry that neutralizes intellectual thoughts within the body's cerebral circuitry;

eka template: subtle circuitry that sustains geometric codes and modulates the language of light; facilitates alchemy of conscious mastery;

el shaddai: garment of light; merkabah; physics of creation in its purest form;

electrokinesis: generate and control electrical currents through the use of the mind; recharge or transfiguration of electricity from electronically-based devices;

electromagnetic energy field: subtle energy field that encompasses all bodies of light; living essence of yin-yang frequencies;

electromagnetic template: subtle circuitry that sustains the grid of light for the human circuit system;

electron particle spin: energetic momentum of particles in the main power current of our spinal column that transfigures our frequency; light in the center of the vesica piscis, a sacred symbol for 2 overlapping discs of light;

eli, eli, eli: body of zohar; opens primary chakratic circuitry;

elohim: interstellar frequency of our consciousness that lives between space and time; guards intergalactic portals;

emissaries of light: our light, as in archangels;

emotion: energy-in-motion; desires obscured by fictions of the mind; state of consciousness that causes reaction or response;

energy: resonant frequencies of light; microcosmic-macrocosmic life force;

energy-in-motion: release of cellular memory that ignites energetic feelings; emotion;

energy patterns: vibrational frequencies that energetically solidify;

enlightenment: movement into the light; full conscious knowing of all things;

enochian: intergalactic civilization in the galactic core;

epi-kinetic template: subtle circuitry that sustains a centrifugal geometric force, which ignites the electron particle spin within the circuit system;

esh ka eem: kabbalistic tree of life;

eternal: always existing, perpetual, without beginning or end;

eternity: indefinable vastness of light throughout creation;

etheric: invisible life force based in the interstellar substance ether; decoded intuition through experiential feelings; realm of multidimensional consciousness;

etheric template: subtle circuitry that maintains the foundational grid of light for all the templates;

evolution: process of spiritual growth through human development;

existence: state of being; universal order; momentum that carries the flow of life;

fountain of creativity: creation of full potential;

free will: bestows free choice according to one's accord; option to do whatever one wishes regardless of whether it is for the highest good of all concerned;

frequency: fundamental conductor and building block of the universe; number of cycles in energetic oscillating waves of light; vibrations per mono-second as in momentum of the electron particle spin;

resonant frequency: any innate frequency of light;

unified frequency: emanation of oneness as a frequency of light;

vibrational frequency: wavelengths; wave of energy that flows throughout our physical body; electrical charge within atoms, molecules and cells;

fusion: act of merging; that which is greater than the sum of its parts; light within unified consciousness;

future self: our light within intergalactic consciousness; merged aspect of consciousness;

galactic: another galaxy or universe; pertaining to form without form;

galactic core: portal for intergalactic consciousness; central sun for all universes; center for intergalactic consciousness; frequency of light that nourishes the earth's sun; pulsates it cosmic cadence through the solar heart; cosmic eye of this solar system; synergizes the interstellar frequency of the galactic lightbody into our circuit system;

galactic houses of spirit: infinite astrological configurations; also known as the house of many mansions;

galaxy: complex network of interrelated star systems isolated from similar systems by vast regions of space; comprises subatomic particles within and between billions of stars; large system of stars held together by gravitation;

garment of el shaddai: divinity within unified consciousness;

gaweah: galactic lightbody;

geburah: middle sefirah of the feminine triad;

gematrian template: subtle circuitry that synergizes our light, as shekinah; sustains mathematical codes of sacred geometry;

geokineis: alteration of mineral composition; natural release of energy between tectonic plates;

geometric codes: interstellar codes of light; 12 configurations of light in original dna;

golden age: age of light; unified continuum of no-time and no-space;

gold-platinum light: resonant pulsation of light that amplifies the electron particle spin in the central meridian of the spinal column; highest frequency of light that our physical body can synergize in the 3rd dimension;

grand sextile: astrological configuration of 6 aspects of 60 degrees each, known as sextiles, that form a star of david;

grid system: geometric blueprint of interstellar frequencies of light; electrical energetic grid around earth; ley lines;

gyrokinesis: realignment of gravitational fields of energy;

hexahedron: platonic solid; sustains a frequency that quickens the ascension experience in each of us;

higher self: oversoul; christ-light; our consciousness as it weaves in and out of other timelines;

hod: sefirah at the bottom of the feminine triad;

hologram: 3 dimensional holographic image of realities created from experiences of duality and polarity; projection of thoughts and beliefs into linear time and space; images from a split laser beam;

hydrokinesis: alter liquid such as water, oil and alcohol; increase or decrease in the momentum of water;

I AM: divine blueprint; "I" is the witnessing presence within unified consciousness and "AM" is all-that-is witnessing itself; covenant of light between the human self, higher self and all-that-is; blossoming evolution of soul;

icosa-dodecahedron: energetically blends water with the interstellar substance ether; geometric air-based solid of pentagons and triangles that sustain an advanced interstellar frequency of light;

icosahedron: platonic solid; aspect of a merged frequency that supports the new matrix of life;

incarnate: embodiment of soul into the atoms, molecules, and cells of a living form;

inclusion: life in unity and wholeness;

individuation: soul in human embodiment;

infrared light: an invisible part of the spectrum of light; comprises electromagnetic radiations of wavelengths from 0.8 to 1000 microns;

interdimensional: access to all dimensions within self;

interdimensional timeline: stream of consciousness that sustains parallel or alternate realities;

intergalactic: life within star systems, galaxies and universes;

intergalactic consciousness: resonant pulsations of consciousness within interplanetary civilizations;

intergalactic federation: upholds an intelligent system of cosmic organization that functions under a doctrine of non-interference; as this consciousness we are the ashtar command, a fleet of space commanders that oversee and govern all activities between interplanetary civilizations in this and other regions of distant universes;

intergalactic tongues: sacred tongues spoken within other interplanetary civilizations;

integration: organization of the integral whole; fusion of the innate principle of knowing;

interplanetary civilizations: our consciousness in other universes, galaxies and their star systems;

interstellar: between or among the stars;

intrastellar: within or inside a star or stars;

interstellar elixir: cosmic cadence in the solar heart; pulsation of our own cosmic rhythm;

interstellar sefirot: spiritual vessel of infinite light; bridges human consciousness with the star systems in earth's galaxy;

intuition: feeling the compass within the sea of life; response in terms of wholeness and synthesis;

kabbalah: mystical tradition and teaching of judiasm; tree of life that interconnects human consciousness with ain soph or;

karma: principle of cause and effect; denotes consequences of deeds from lifetimes of incarnations; repetitive programs; what one sows, one reaps;

kether: sefirah at the top of the triad of balance;

key: energetic experience of accelerating frequencies designed to facilitate conscious ascension;

kingdom of heaven: unified continuum of infinite love; energetic presence within you;

knowing: remembrance of intergalactic consciousness; realization of all that we are within all-that-is;

kuchavim: our consciousness as the council of 24 elders; 12 sets of galactic twin flames that administer cosmic order directly through ain soph or to the star system sirius;

language of light: star codes, sacred geometry, sound, color and configurations of energy; intergalactic tongues;

layooesh shekinah: light within; feminine principle; androgyny;

lemurian scrolls: ancient sacred text from the civilization of lemuria;

levitation: state of awareness through which we defy gravity and suspend our physical bodies in the air; form of telekinesis;

lifestream: soul in embodiment; our resonance of light in other interplanetary civilizations; consciousness as it weaves throughout dimensions, star systems and universes; uses the astrological signs of the zodiac as the highway for incarnation;

light: a particle; waves of frequencies; illumination; radiant electromagnetic waves of energy; rainbow spectrum; gleam or sparkle in the eyes;

lightbody: interstellar body of light that surrounds each lifestream; merkabah; perfected interstellar blueprint; ageless and luminous;

light year: distance that light travels in 1 solar year, about 5,880,000,000,000 miles; unit for measuring stellar distance;

logoic template: frequency of light that synergizes knowing;

magnetics: energy that attracts or repels;

magnetism: energetically channel the flow of resonant frequencies throughout the physical body;

magnokinesis: create and transfigure electromagnetic grids;

malkuth: sefirah at the bottom of the triad of balance;

manna: spiritual nourishment; interstellar substance;

masters: communion of our consciousness; full conscious knowing;

matrix (matrices) of light: energetic projections of holographic light that solidifies through conscious intention; grids of light that sustain interstellar substance; facsimile of dimensional templates modulated into matrices of light; transfigures the core of each atom, molecule and cell of all life; geometric matrices in our own resonance of light;

matter: density within material form; substance that relates to form and occupies space;

medulla oblongata: lowest part of the brain; energetically connected to the central meridian of the spinal column;

melchizedek priesthood: ancient spiritual order of cosmic intelligence;

merkabah: interstellar garment for the body of light; garment of light or galactic lightbody;

meshiah m'shi shi: frequency of light that enters the physical body through the 8th chakratic gateway; christ-light;

microcosmic-macrocosmic: in-breath and out-breath of life force;

monadic template: subtle circuitry that protects the sacred knowledge of soul's evolution and sustains it within the hall of akashic records;

mono-seconds: vibrational cycles equal to 1 billionth of a second;

multidimensional consciousness: our light within earth's star system, galaxy and other universes;

netzach: sefirah at the bottom of the masculine triad;

new matrix of life: multidimensional state of consciousness; 5th dimension;

nibiru: planet of reptilian civilizations, known as nibiruans;

north node of the moon: point in the orbital path of earth's moon that sustains the frequency of potentiality;

octahedron: platonic solid that has 8 sides;

octave of light: spectrum of light; sustains planetary harmonics of sound and brain wave frequencies;

off-planet: experiences that occur outside the sphere of earth;

omnigalactic source: 13th sefirah on the galactic tree of life; galactic center of unified consciousness;

omnipresent: being present; enveloping presence both within and without;

oneness: universal synthesis with all life; our resonance of light as ain soph or;

orion: stellar constellation; assimilates our consciousness within the structural organization of the intergalactic federation; our consciousness in this civilization works in units of group souls and supports the purpose of our cosmic mission;

oversoul: etheric presence; subtle circuitry for thousands of tiny threads of light that energetically hold the electromagnetic energy field together;

oversoul template: subtle circuitry that supports conscious communion of christ-light;

paradigm: age of light;

old paradigm: cycle of linear time; particular program of thoughts, beliefs, emotions; limitation as a result of conditioned programming; structure that no longer serves its original purpose;

new paradigm: cycle of spherical time; new matrix of life that reflects liberation, sovereignty, equality, balance and harmony;

parallel reality: reality within interdimensional timelines; realities of consciousness that recycle in accordance with their own momentum; multiple realities within consciousness that are parallel to experiences in life;

pentagrammaton: blueprint of the tetragrammaton;

perfection: state of being; highest degree of excellence; the nothing and the everything simultaneously;

photokinesis: creates and alters light; transmutes light and changes its colors; shifts the light spectrum; invisibility at will;

photon belt: an interstellar region of increased photonic light; progressive frequencies of light that vibrate to a megahertz that is much higher than human life has ever experienced on earth; 2000 year cycle;

physiological circuitry: elemental holding vessel for the unified circuit system; reflects spiritual aspects in the circuit system that are cosmic in nature;

piscean age: patriarchal age; belief in externalized divinity; previous to the age of aquarius or 7th golden age;

planetary logos: assimilates interstellar encodements into earth's grid; synergizes advanced technologies within consciousness; scans potentialities; transfigures energy so that it is compatible with earth's new atmosphere; sustains the key to earth's evolution;

platonic solids: 5 geometric figures that share common characteristics in that all sides are equal and all angles and faces are identical;

pleiades: star system in earth's galaxy; known as seven sisters; intergalactic civilization known as the pleiadians;

polarity: dualistic opposites such as light or dark;

polarization: external reference through thought or language; creates dualistic opposites; trapped consciousness;

portal: entry points on earth that receive and transmit cosmic frequencies; stargate to intergalactic consciousness;

potential: capable of being; state of conscious creation; fountain of creativity;

precognition: ability to know events before they occur;

psychokinesis: alter energy, matter, vibration and recorded times; comprises the full range of kinetic ability to greater or lesser degrees;

pyrokinesis: control of extreme hot temperatures; wave lengths of frequencies that create temperature increases in all forms of matter; create and direct fire at will;

quantum shift: transfiguration in the mechanics of physics applicable to the atomic and nuclear level of human consciousness and form;

rays of divine will: higher rays of consciousness;

rays of perspective: first 7 of the 12 rays in the spectrum of light that emanates from ain soph or;

record keepers: guard the knowledge of star systems and galaxies; record the mythology of earth, which includes life on the continent mu, lemurian tablets and its scrolls;

remote viewing: projection from a single physical location that views a 3D event, as it occurs within the unified continuum;

rendezvous: meeting place and time for souls to complete prearranged agreements; specific timeframe, or place, for the purpose of reconciliation;

resonance: vibrations of different frequencies on the same wavelength; fundamental conductor and building block of the universe; inner vibrations activated in response to an external stimulus;

resurrection: awakening from an unconscious state into full conscious awareness;

7th golden age: age of aquarius; sustains multidimensional consciousness;

sacred geometry: foundation or building blocks for geometric encodements; blueprints;

second-coming: inner resurrection of christ-light; erroneous religious belief;

sefirah: 1 of 10 spiritual branches on the sefirot (tree of life); garment of light that emanates our light, as an archangel;

sefirot: kabbalistic tree of life; energetic bridge between all consciousness; spiritual vessel through which ain soph or manifests within form;

self: uniting principle as soul; our light within unified consciousness;

self-identity: identification with individual self; attachment to who we are as form;

separation: energetic division within consciousness; self-created split from all that we are as source;

seraphim: as seraphim, our light emanates from the highest order of angels and transmits the flame of infinite love directly from ain soph or;

seven kumaras: 7 aspects of our consciousness on venus;

shadow: concealed piece within self that seeks resolution; dark night of soul;

shalusch: seeds of divinity; androgynous principles of yhvh and shekinah; pulsates as the divine harmonics of creation; trinitized capstone of the tetrahedron;

shamballa: return of celestial paradise; denotes heaven is on the new earth; serves as headquarters for the living masters who reside on earth;

shape shift: alter from one form to another;

shekinah: androgynous feminine principle that is soph;

sirius: star system in earth's galaxy; lightbody for the 3rd dimension; transmits geometric codes from the language of light into our awareness; stores the remembrance of human experience as imprints, which are then transferred to the akashic records;

solar gateway: frequency of light; cone-shaped energy; located in the main power current in the central meridian of the spinal column; superimposes central nervous system; frequency that intertwines with cerebral circuitry in the brain; primes basic chakratic system for assimilation of subtle circuitry;

solar heart: energetic distributor of light; sustains the interstellar elixir of infinite love; cosmic cadence that emanates from the galactic core or central sun; cosmic cadence, as our own pulsating rhythm, located behind and to the right of the physical heart; interstellar frequency of the unified heart within consciousness; sacred inner chamber of light where we energetically feel heightened states of awareness; emanates infinite light through the one heart within all creation;

solar logos: implements the divine plan for earth; oversees all areas of cosmic governance; interprets energetic patterns from an intergalactic perspective; facilitates sovereignty on earth;

soul: resonance of light within the breath of first creation; evolving spark of light; directs human ego to conscious mastery according to contracts in its divine blueprint; invincible spark of creation; inner reflection of wholeness;

soulmate: mother, father, siblings, friends, lovers, business associates coming together to complete unresolved energetic patterns; contracts arranged between souls prior to incarnation;

soul-spark: fiery core of inner light; twin-ray frequency;

soul-star: energetic gateway 6 - 12 inches above the crown of the head;

south node of the moon: point in the orbital path of earth's moon; frequency of attained wisdom and innate abilities;

sovereignty: state of divine grace; conscious state of authentic dominion; being whole and complete within yourself;

spoken word: covenant of light that alters matter; declaration of the language of light made manifest through intention; spoken word I AM reflects self-actualization, sovereignty and freedom;

star codes: sustain geometric encodements of cosmic intelligence that energetically transmit interstellar frequencies through a grid of light; activate our consciousness and transfigure genetic composition;

star of david: configuration of light; configuration of a 6-pointed star formed of 2 equilateral triangles so that the base of each triangle bisects 2 sides of the other; spiritual symbology for androgynous masculine and feminine; jewish symbol, the mogan david [dovid];

stargate: interstellar portal into other star systems, galaxies and universes;

star system: stellar system; groupings of stars, planets, moons and other cosmic phenomena that orbit within a gravitational field of energy

starseeds: our light as it emanates throughout many universes; germinate intergalactic seeds, synergize dna of each root race and birth into individualized form; align the earth with the divine plan; facilitate in the synergy of intergalactic communication and assimilate it as conscious knowing; incarnate into 3rd dimensional reality and act as a cosmic anchor for the ascension experience;

subtle circuitry: grid system comprised of templates;

synchronicity: energetic current through which we experience the flow of life with ease and grace; solidifies the intersection of all parallel realities as they occur in the same moment; experience of realities that are parallel to every moment;

synergize: conscious intention that uses light for transfiguration;

synergy: unified experience of light; an inward perception of expansion within multidimensional realities;

synthesis: fusion of separation within consciousness; unified experience of wholeness, as in universal synthesis;

synthesize: conscious intention that fuses separation;

tantra: ultimate sexual union;

tapestry: intricately woven threads of consciousness; sustains the primary curriculum that magnetically attracts; threads of consciousness that crisscross over and under other timelines; woven by soul to form a specific web of life;

telekinesis: alter gravity and electromagnetics; movement of physical objects within their present location as well as at a distance;

telepathy: energetic exchange of cosmic intelligence with resonant frequencies in this and other interplanetary civilizations; communication that transcends the 5 senses, such as thought transmission;

teleportation: ability to instantaneously travel from one location to another; form that dematerializes and rematerializes at will, and travels throughout multiple interplanetary civilizations; assimilation of magnetic and electromagnetic frequencies of light;

template: fixed pattern of light; basis from which frequencies modulate patterns of light and create individualized matrices through conscious intention; geometric design;

temple of light: sacred space; inner temple where we energetically experience our light as ain soph or;

tetragrammaton: consists of the letters yod, hey, vav, hey; yhvh;

tetrahedron: the capstone shalusch; sustains interstellar codes within the codon of the original configuration of dna;

thermokinesis: generate warmth and heat; alteration of objective or subjective temperature;

thoughtforms: energetic patterns of thought that weave in and out of consciousness;

threads of consciousness: cords of attachment from experiences in interdimensional timelines;

timelines: multidimensional planes of existence; realities that change according to density;

time-space continuum: time and space where all the multiplicities of time are experienced simultaneously;

tiphereth: upper middle sefirah in the triad of balance;

transcend: expand beyond limits; rise above as in transcend limiting beliefs and thoughts;

transfiguration: quantum shift, as in resurrection; meltdown of density within physiological circuitry; shift of the physical body to the refined lightbody;

transformation: change in form, appearance and character;

transmute: transform from one state into another;

transmutation: change to another state of awareness; experiential process that purifies, heals and perfects;

tree of life: matrix of light that reveals the progression of human evolution as it strives to attain conscious understanding of itself, as creation;

twin flame: identical electronic blueprint of our soul;

twin-ray: resonant frequency of our own light;

ultraviolet light: beyond the known spectrum of light;

unified circuit system: complex grid system that infuses with the meridians of our physical body through the central nervous system to the brain; functions as a unit of wholeness to balance our body's electric, magnetic and subtle systems; includes physiological circuitry, cerebral-emotional circuitry, chakratic circuitry, subtle circuitry and the galactic lightbody; a reference point for the stabilization process, which supports the final, yet essential phase of inner communion;

unified consciousness: frequency of inner communion, rather than a reference to the frequency of many; communion of our consciousness in all galaxies and universes;

unified continuum: multiplicities of no-time and no-space experienced simultaneously;

unified energy field: closed circuit system, as in frequency of beloved complement;

unified rays of light: resonant frequencies of light that emanate from ain soph or;

universe: totality of all things; creation; macrocosm of heavenly bodies of light;

universal law: organization of cosmic law; sustains equality, balance and synchronicity; beyond all limitations;

veils: energetic patterns that create fragmentation within the circuit system; reinforces the experience of limitation; prevents the ability to attain full consciousness;

vesica piscis: sacred symbol for 2 overlapping discs of light that amplify the electron particle spin;

vibration: energy that is experienced both from within or without; oscillation of movement;

vibrations per mono-second: measurement of frequencies in the electron particle spin; 1 mono-second is equal to 1 billionth of a second;

violet flame: transmutes all dissonance and brings balance into the circuit system; activates the temple of peace; energetic technology that supports transmutation of imbalanced energy;

vitakinesis: alter life force within the kingdom of nature;

vril: atlantean sacred tongue; language of light; cosmic energy at the base of the spine;

wisdom: quality or state of being wise; knowledge of what is true; conscious enlightenment; discernment; insight;

yesod: lower middle sefirah in the triad of balance;

yhsvh: frequency of light; union of yhvh and shekinah; unified consciousness;

yhvh: tetragrammaton; sacred name for god; derived from jehovah; androgynous masculine and feminine principles within ain soph or;

yod: fire letter in the hebrew alphabet;

zero point: point of neutrality;

zohar template: subtle circuitry that synergizes our light, as yhvh;

Ordering Information

This book is available through:

Outskirts Press, Inc.
10940 S. Parker Rd. - 515
Parker, CO 80134

(888) OP.BOOKS
Call 1.888.672.6657 toll free,
fax: 888.208.8601

e-mail: info@outskirtspress.com
www.outskirtspress.com

www.HeavenOnEarthInternational.com

Soon to be released:

CD of book: *Experience Heaven on Earth: The New Matrix of Life*

CD: Energetic Keys from the book *Experience Heaven on Earth*

All CD Products are recorded by *Salantra*